"John Renesch, renowned futurist and prolific author, has written a deeply provocative book to inspire the evolution of a new humanity. *The Great Growing Up* brilliantly captures the critical importance of the present moment and outlines a trajectory for achieving a mature, peaceful future for all. John's roadmap to our collective future is clear, compelling, and transformative. His new book is important and empowering. I highly recommend it."

— Lynne Twist, co-founder, The Pachamama Alliance

"Like a master painter, John Renesch provides a broad interpretive mural of the last half-century along with a sweeping and sense-making depiction of how humankind has encumbered itself with less than a fully human milieu. But he does not leave us in stoicism or anomie. He encourages hope that we can rebuild our future through new forms of conscious leadership. One is left with both an understanding of our past and a renewed sense of mission regarding a future on which mankind's very survival depends."

— Andre L. Delbecq, J. Thomas and Kathleen L. McCarthy University Professor, Santa Clara University

"John Renesch is a Renaissance Man who lives in the twenty-first century. In *The Great Growing Up* he shows how, through conscious evolution, we can put our predatory past behind us and create a dignitarian world. Prophetic yet practical, *The Great Growing Up* integrates science, philosophy, spirituality, and psychology into a compelling vision of a world that will work for everyone."

— Robert W. Fuller, former president, Oberlin College, author of *All Rise: Somebodies, Nobodies, and the Politics of Dignity*

"This book is about the art of the possible despite all odds in these turbulent times. It is a manifesto for all of us as humans to lead rather than follow our own evolution."

— Mark Thompson, bestselling coauthor of *Success Built to Last*

"In his new book—*The Great Growing Up*—John Renesch challenges us with authority, humanity, energy and optimism, to address the key issues facing society today, both globally and personally—and these two dimensions are closely linked. It is full of valuable insights, as well as being a call to action. These messages need urgent attention if we are to survive this century, let alone see a better world in the years ahead. Time is not on our side."

— Bruce Lloyd, Emeritus Professor of Strategic Management, London South Bank University

"Ever the optimistic realist, John Renesch makes clear from the beginning that *The Great Growing Up* intends to make us uncomfortable with the lies we tell ourselves about our world and our place in it. In debunking the myths that we think guide us, John offers a transformative manifesto of what is possible for humanity with the emphasis on "human." But this is not new age mumbo jumbo; John's background in business and the physical sciences is evident throughout. Read this book and share it."

– James A. Autry, author of *The Servant Leader* and *Looking Around for God*

"In *The Great Growing Up*, John Renesch meticulously describes today's dysfunctional societies and the dissatisfactions they have created. However, a well-functioning society is possible through 'conscious evolution,' the use of human intention to create alternative money systems, transformative learning, gender parity, energy independence, and a host of other paradigm changes. *The Great Growing Up* contains a vivid description of contemporary society that is as accurate as it is depressing; however, Renesch gives his readers a 'Great Dream' for the future that is rooted in the writings of the founders of the United States, yet rebooted for the tattered world of the 21st century . . . a splendid book."

– Stanley Krippner, Ph.D., Professor of Psychology, Saybrook University, co-author of *Personal Mythology*

"John Renesch has been a pioneer and visionary in the search for human values based on reciprocity and relationship rather than self interest and dominance. His search has led him to the threshold of a new awareness that he aptly calls *The Great Growing Up*. His book is an invitation to cross that threshold and together remake the world."

– Alan Briskin, author of *The Stirring of Soul in the Workplace* and coauthor of *The Power of Collective Wisdom*

"John's thinking and work about the direction we humans have to take is both challenging and timely. In *The Great Growing Up* we are given authentic hope. This book provides both an analysis and template for deep contemplation and action."

– David Kyle, author of *The Four Powers of Leadership*

"Inspiring, practical and thought provoking . . . *The Great Growing Up* challenges each of us to develop and stretch our capacities to generate a global reality that secures a preferred future 'that works for everyone'."

– Angeles Arrien, Ph.D., cultural anthropologist, author of *The Four-Fold Way* and *Second Half of Life*

"Have you ever wondered whether our planet is engaged in some epic transition to a better society? One where individuals, due to massive new technological and social interdependences, come to see themselves as part of a single integrated 'organism' or 'global brain,' as well as free, individual moral actors? Teilhard de Chardin called this coming event 'Planetization' and some foresight scholars see it as part of the natural developmental future of Earth. If we are to responsibly integrate our incredible new powers for self- and environmental change, and protect against ongoing environmental degradation and destruction, such a consciousness shift must occur. Read this sublime book, and start being the change yourself, every day. You'll find very few routes to deeper universal insight, peace and happiness that are as direct and valuable as this book."

   – John Smart, President, Acceleration Studies Foundation

"John Renesch is not only a smart man, but also a wise one. *The Great Growing Up* offers a conscious choice for the kind of future we want to create and the role we each want to play in bringing it about. Don't just read this book—do it!"

   – Alan M. Webber, cofounder, *Fast Company* magazine

"*The Great Growing Up* gives us vital and wise guidelines to the unprecedented emergence of ourselves as cocreators of our world. It is an important work for our own conscious evolution, self and social."

   – Barbara Marx Hubbard, founder, Foundation for Conscious Evolution

"In *The Great Growing Up*, John Renesch has given us an astute diagnosis of what ails us as individuals and as a global community. He then gives us a prescription for treatment. But rather than a bitter pill to swallow, we have a recipe filled with hope for a renewed spirit."

   – Gregg Magrane, Ph.D., geneticist, University of California San Francisco

"In *The Great Growing Up* John Renesch has brought together an impressive range of sources to provide a readable overview of our prospects for a renewed civilization. He manages to capture the essence of many concepts and ideas and to make them accessible. You don't need a Ph.D. to read this book—merely an open mind and a willing spirit."

   – Richard Slaughter, futurist, Foresight International, Brisbane, Australia

"This is a beautiful easy-to-read book. Renesch weaves together the external and inner challenges humanity faces—ageing, inequity, gender imbalances, spiritual poverty, lack of reflection—and provides us with solutions forward. Humanity is like an adolescent, the transition to adulthood is not always easy, but through the work of John Renesch we are given an exploratory map on how this could be possible, and even more important, his book provides us with a pause, a time to reflect, on how each one of us can play a role in the transformation ahead, now."
   – Professor Sohail Inayatullah, Tamkang University, Taiwan and the University of the Sunshine Coast, Australia

"The American Dream is under siege instead of being seized and society is at a significant crossroads. *The Great Growing Up* not only warns us of the destructive path our world is heading down, it provides a vision for a brighter, better future that our children can inherit. The good news is that we are still in control: we each can make a difference and John Renesch shows us how."
   – Brian Feinblum, Planned Television Arts, Chief Marketing Officer, VP

"John Renesch challenges us to examine where we are in our evolution and squarely face the challenges confronting us as a species. Then he offers us the opportunity to transcend our conditions and engage in a global transformation of epic proportions. Will we squander this opportunity or act on it? Provocative, engaging and, most importantly, essential to the conscious evolution of humankind."
   – Ken Dychtwald, Ph.D., best-selling author of sixteen books, including *With Purpose: From Success to Significance in Work and Life*

"I welcome this important book which maps the unprecedented challenges and opportunities for humanity in this era. John Renesch, as always, is an expert guide to this phase of human development and he lays out our options with deep understanding and compassion."
   – Hazel Henderson, President, Ethical Markets Media (USA and Brazil), author of *Ethical Markets: Growing The Green Economy* and *Beyond Globalization*

"Once again, John Renesch gives us the benefit of his accumulated wisdom and experience with *The Great Growing Up*. He points the way to a new vision of infinite possibilities, which is available to everyone. If you're interested in changing the world for the better, then *The Great Growing Up* is a must read. You'll be glad you did!"
   – Michael Toms, Founding President, New Dimensions Radio; author of the bestselling *An Open Life: Joseph Campbell in Conversation with Michael Toms* and *True Work: Doing What You Love and Loving What You Do*

"In his new book, *The Great Growing Up,* John Renesch explodes the myths that have kept us bound to a dying world and awakens us—our minds and spirits—to the new possibilities. His deep reflections help us regain our inherent balance between how we choose to use the resources of the world and the resources of the spirit within—choices which allow us to 'take a stand,' standing on both feet, and walk into a new and more alive world. Congratulations on creating a really excellent book for our time!"

– Pat Lynch, Founder and CEO, Women's Online Media and Education Network

"*The Great Growing Up* invites you into an inspiring, big-picture vision of a world healed by changes in how we think, work, and live as individuals. John Renesch stands with you before the mirror of time to examine what we have created through our sometimes unconscious, careless *freedoms*. He plants seeds of change in the process, creating a space for you to discover a deeper sense of contribution through your own personal transformation into *The Great Growing Up* the world badly needs."

– Debbe Kennedy, founder, Global Dialogue Center and Leadership Solutions Companies, author of *Putting Our Differences to Work: The Fastest Way to Innovation, Leadership, and High Performance*

"In his new book, John Renesch makes an insightful and honest assessment of our past and maps the way forward for us as a society and individuals. His call to action is both critical and timely, empowering each of us to create the world we can be proud of—unified, just and profoundly human. The wealth of information and wisdom that is contained in this book is amazing."

– Julia Balandina Jaquier, Ph.D., Head of Sustainable Investment Group, AIG Investments, Zurich

"A powerful visionary beacon for our evolving humanity. John Renesch shows us how to be the change we would like to see—in humanity."

– Debashis Chowdhury, author of *In Our Own Image: Humanity's Quest for Divinity via Technology*

"With so many of us struggling, we all need a vision of hope that looks at life, business and the dark side of human behavior right in the eye. That's what John Renesch does in this provocative, comprehensive guide to the future—and our role in constructing it."

– Patricia Aburdene, author: *Megatrends 2010: The Rise of Conscious Capitalism*

OTHER BOOKS AUTHORED OR COMPILED BY JOHN RENESCH

Steven's Choice

Getting to the Better Future: A Matter of Conscious Choosing

Leadership in a New Era

New Traditions in Business

Setting Goals

The New Entrepreneurs (with Michael Ray)

The New Bottom Line: Bringing Heart and Soul to Business
(with Bill DeFoore)

Rediscovering the Soul of Business (with Bill DeFoore)

Learning Organizations (with Sarita Chawla)

Working Together: Producing Synergy by Honoring Diversity
(ed., Angeles Arrien)

Intuition at Work: Pathways to Unlimited Possibilities
(eds., Roger Frantz and Alex Pattakos)

Community Building: Renewing Spirit & Learning in Business
(ed., Kaz Gozdz)

When the Canary Stops Singing (ed., Pat Barrentine)

To Bruce – with best wishes!
John Renesch

THE GREAT GROWING UP

Being Responsible for Humanity's Future

John Renesch

HOHM PRESS
PRESCOTT, ARIZONA

Cover Design: Accurance, Bloomington, Illinois

Interior Design and Layout: Kubera Graphics, Becky Fulker, Prescott, Arizona

Library of Congress Cataloging-in-Publication Data

Renesch, John, 1937-
  The great growing up : being responsible for humanity's future / John Renesch.
    p. cm.
  Includes bibliographical references and index.
  ISBN 978-1-935387-18-3 (trade paper : alk. paper)
  1. Human ecology. 2. Social ecology. 3. Human evolution. 4. Social evolution. 5. Social ethics. 6. Environmental policy. I. Title.
  GF50.R465 2011
  304.2--dc23
                    2011025801

HOHM PRESS
P.O. Box 2501
Prescott, AZ 86302
800-381-2700
http://www.hohmpress.com

This book was printed in the U.S.A. on recycled, acid-free paper using soy ink.

CONTENTS

PREFACE

There are two windows of opportunity for human beings in motion right now. One is closing fast while the other is slowly opening wider. The one that's closing fast is made up of all the threats to the quality of life as we know it—deforestation, population growth, deteriorating water and air quality, and all the other trends that make headlines each day. When this window closes, human beings may have to make one of the toughest mass adjustments in history if our species is to survive. This is the window of bad news.

The window that is opening is the good news: ever-increasing numbers of individuals seeking self-actualization, growing in consciousness, and willing to take on leadership roles in bringing about the first conscious evolution of our species. This window represents a somewhat invisible global movement of historic proportions. This collective choice is choosing adulthood over the largely adolescent ways we have been relating to one another and to our planet Earth.

Just about every system we have created—economic, government, healthcare, international security, education—is in crisis. At their best these systems are dysfunctional, and at their worst they're doing more harm than good. The signs are too obvious to ignore. It's time to grow up and be responsible as adults for what we have created as adolescents.

The Great Growing Up shows us how we can make this historic transition while both windows of opportunity are open.

PERSONAL NOTE

My earliest motivation in life was to assure the survival of my younger brother and myself. I was thrust into the role of "head of household" after barely starting school in the post World War II years, with a brother four years behind me. At the time, survival looked like maintaining the remnants of a family, making sure my kid brother and I got fed and wore clean clothes and that my mother was taken care of when she was drunk, which was almost every night and weekend. Luckily, our mother managed to hold down a daytime job, so we had some money. I could wake her from her stupor, get her signature on a check, shop for groceries and fill in the amount. Not bad for a pre-ten-year-old kid!

When my mother remarried and it became apparent that our family home would be stable, I began to relax about mere survival and looked around to see what the rest of the world was doing. I was now in my mid-to-late teens, having skipped most of my childhood and taken on what I understood "grown-up behavior" to be.

After a decade or two of entrepreneurial adventures—starting businesses that looked like fun to me—I started growing out of my own egocentric ways and began experiencing the entire world. Well into my thirties, I started identifying with the pain and suffering I saw in the news and, sometimes, in my own communities. As I became interested in developing as a person, in getting to know myself and growing emotionally and spiritually, I somehow learned to distinguish between the feelings I was taking on from others, through empathy, and my own emotions. This was enormously helpful and lightened my emotional burdens whenever I confused the two.

At last it felt safe to feel love for everybody. By this time I was almost fifty.

This was also when my work became a calling, when my purpose found me. *The Great Growing Up* is the culmination of my work for the past quarter century. But I did not get here by myself. I must thank many people for their support and wisdom.

ACKNOWLEDGMENTS

First, let me thank some of my heroes—people who have inspired and influenced me positively, some still living, and others who have passed on. These people include thought leaders, authors, futurists, social scientists, spiritual leaders, champions of transformation everywhere, friends and teachers, my health professionals, philosophers, public servants, social entrepreneurs, the founders of the United States of America, and the many inspirational leaders from all over the world.

I am so grateful to my parents, Jack and Ellen, for giving me life so I could have this incredible ride. And what a ride it is! My father gave me his family name, which seems to have run its course, given that I may now be the last Renesch left on Earth. My mother gave me many qualities of character that I cherish.

Much appreciation and love also goes to my stepfather, Joseph Ruebel, for his contribution to my family's stability when it really mattered.

I also want to acknowledge my sole biological sibling, Bob Ruebel, for whom I was a surrogate father in early childhood. Knowing nothing about parenting, I did the best I could with what I knew at the age of seven or eight. I love him today as much as I did then.

A huge thank you goes to my maternal grandparents, Henry and Wilhelmina Dusterberry, for their love, and for doing all they could to make up for a difficult situation in my childhood.

Much appreciation goes to all those colleagues who have supported me by proofreading and editing my many articles, op-ed pieces and editorials over the years.

Thanks to all my business clients—those who have booked me for keynote talks as well as those I have coached or mentored over the years. You've helped me grow into my "elder" status, and learn as well. I love the reciprocity! My versatile life in business prior to becoming a futurist (or whatever you call me these days) has been blessed by you all.

From my motorsports' days in the 1950s and 1960s, my work as an event organizer through the 1970s, involvement in real estate and investment securities in the 1980s, my shift to the published word and social transformation in the 1990s, and all those ventures—for profit and not-for-profit—amongst and between, thanks to *everyone* with whom I've worked.

It's been over fifty years of fun and challenges, heartache and elation, great successes and heartbreaking failures, fellowship and discord. For those with whom things ended harmoniously, as well as for those with whom things ended otherwise, thank you all for the learning and the experience.

I am also incredibly grateful for my relationship with God, my Higher Power. I definitely have a very intimate relationship with both the feminine and masculine face of the divine and feel gratitude each day for my physical life, my spiritual life, the wonderful people in my life and my surroundings. I am truly blessed.

Also, I wish to thank those scholars, authors, researchers and theorists whose work I have found valuable and are referenced in these pages. As a self-confessed nonscholar who lacks the temperament to dig for so much information, I truly appreciate the work you've all done that allows me access to your wisdom. I hope you feel I've treated it with the respect it deserves.

Thanks to all those people who looked over early drafts of this manuscript and offered their comments, including my colleagues who penned advance words of praise. I have much gratitude for Faith Kuczaj and her early editing support and for my agents Bill Gladstone and David Nelson at Waterside Productions and their efforts on my behalf. A special thanks also to Jackie Miller, Tom Eddington and Partnerships for Change for their support in getting this book out there in the world. I especially wish to thank the people at Hohm Press—Dasya Zuccarello, Regina Sara Ryan, and Bala Zuccarello—who worked with me in the final birthing of this work.

INTRODUCTION

What do the experts predict about the future of the world? What is the prognosis for us and the legacy we are leaving to those who follow us?

Regardless of whether the future will be good or bad for the human race, the changes will be happening much more rapidly than in the past. According to Ian Morris, Stanford Professor of Classics and History, there will be much more social development amongst our species in this century: *four times as much*—for better or for worse—as has taken place in the past 15,000 years![1]

The global think tank the Millennium Project reports there is plenty to be hopeful about as well as plenty to concern us. After nine years of research, they tell us, "it has become increasingly clear that humanity has the resources to address its global challenges; what is less clear is how much wisdom, good will, and intelligence we will focus on these challenges." As published in its Executive Overview, the Project states that "we can create the will to act more decisively" in addressing these challenges and "win the race between the increasing proliferation of threats and our increasing ability to improve the human condition."[2] These 2,000 experts from around the world agree that we are in a race and that the outcome is uncertain. But, they affirm, there is hope. *The Great Growing Up* is about building on that hope, pointing to the opportunity we have at this time to tip the scales in favor of making things not only "better," but transcending the existing conditions.

WHO SHOULD READ THIS BOOK?

I offer the following tests for compatibility, since I know what's ahead, and you, dear reader, do not.

The vast majority (nearly seven billion) of us worldwide don't make enough money in one month to buy a book. Many of us could care less about reading anything when every day is focused on finding a scrap of food or a few drops of decent water for our families. So book buyers are a privileged lot, perhaps a single-digit percentage of the global population. Even in "developed" countries only a small minority buys and reads books. This means that you are most likely one of an elite group of privileged people who can read, afford to purchase this book, and have the leisure time *and desire* to read it.

The Great Growing Up is for those who want to see a world that supports human life and allows us all to grow, learn, and have families who feel secure, nurtured and free. If you're feeling so helpless that you've given thought to doing something radical but are not yet committed to it, then read this book. If you feel either so forlorn that you'd like to be lifted out of your misery or are sure that there is a better future waiting for us all, then I invite you to read on.

TAKING RESPONSIBILITY FOR HUMANITY'S FUTURE

I will identify the potential enemies of this transformation to a better world, as well as our allies in making the shift. We are far closer than we may think to the first consciously chosen leap in our evolution.

This book is about taking responsibility for humanity's future by becoming a more conscious *society*. How do we take lessons from all the developments in past decades and apply them to ourselves as a species? How can we all live together? How can we have secure lives in a nurturing environment that is healthy and sustainable, just and neighborly?

The 2008-2009 economic meltdown has taught us that we have been living beyond our material/financial means for quite some time and need to become more fiscally conservative. Simultaneously, we have been living well below our spiritual/emotional means. This book is my attempt to help us get more adventurous and imaginative in the spiritual/emotional aspects of being human.

Before we start, let me clarify something. Much of what is written in these pages might appear to be the thinking of a philosopher or the ramblings of a philosopher wannabe. My background is business and my "on the job training" as a businessman and entrepreneur for several decades taught me pragmatics. My early education was in mathematics and the physical sciences. I consider myself well-grounded. What I portray in this book is completely possible. Whenever I've seen so much possibility for creating something wonderful I'm compelled to go for it. How can I turn my back on such an incredible opportunity?

I urge you to join me as we break free of the straightjacket of established thought and give ourselves the freedom to explore new realms.

ENGAGED OPTIMIST OR RESIGNED PESSIMIST?

While I occasionally get a bit down or despairing about the future of humankind—and the trends can be pretty discouraging—I consider it an occupational hazard. These are the times when I must focus on the optimist inside me and look for the positive that is bringing us to a tipping point—not to a worse future, but to a better one.

Another battle that goes on within me sometimes is whether to repair or transform existing systems and institutions or to move on and consider what new structures would better serve the conscious evolution of our species. We often make dysfunctional institutions stronger and more resistant by trying to change them. Putting our energies into those efforts may be counterproductive. In other words, there frequently comes a point when the more we try to improve them the worse they get! What a downer that could be to cogitate!

One of my heroes is inventor R. Buckminster ("Bucky") Fuller, who writes, "You never change things by fighting existing reality. To change something, build a new model that makes the existing model obsolete."

By feeding the optimist inside me I am able to focus more on the positive vision I have for our future—what I stand FOR—rather than focusing on all the negativity confronting us and being AGAINST that.

Join me in an adventure into some large-scale pragmatic idealism. Let's revive ourselves from our cynical slumber and engage a future beyond anything we thought possible: the Great Dream.

Chapter 1

THE NEW GREAT DREAM

Most people have experienced at least one transcendent moment, perhaps even more than just one; a time when life was so precious, so filled with wonder and awe, the experience was indescribable. While ineffable, the experience can be recalled and relived in the privacy of our own memories. It may have been walking in the woods, during the birth of a baby, being in a state of meditation or some other altered state, or hanging out with a special group of friends where one really feels extraordinarily safe and secure. It was probably quite palpable at the time, like a dizziness or a unique lightness or weightlessness. Perhaps it was a feeling of being connected to everything! And while most of us have had one of these highly personal peak experiences, few of us talk about them. We find them difficult to articulate.

Through the ages, people have yearned for a connection with something beyond themselves, something called by many different names, taking many different shapes. Throughout human existence there has been this quest. It is part of being alive. Let's call this our spiritual dimension. Meanwhile, we live in a material world where we have physical needs. These needs call for our attention, sometimes more strongly than the spiritual and usually with greater immediacy, yet this material dimension cannot be substituted for the spiritual.

We humans are physical beings living in a material world, while yearning for greater connection with our spiritual side. Both dimensions reside within us, one very obvious and one not so conspicuous, one quite visible and tangible and the other invisible and intangible. In fact, just to make it more challenging, the latter is also ineffable. We have trouble verbalizing the spiritual but nonetheless seek it out.

It's interesting how we've dealt with these two dimensions of being human throughout our time on Earth. On occasion, mystics and philosophers have seen the possibility of integrating them and ending this schism of Self. I believe the founders of the United States saw this possibility.

But it has been more popular to pit these two parts against each other, as though one is better, one is worse. In the extreme, this leads us either to some sort of fundamental religious stance and a disowning of the material, or to fundamental materialism with a disowning of the spiritual. Both demonstrate radical fundamentalism in action. Either point of view is like standing on one foot—forcing us to spend an inordinate amount of time and energy struggling to maintain our balance.

While these various ways of compartmentalizing these two dimensions of human existence may be popular, they are artificial. Both insert a boundary between the spiritual and the material dimensions. This boundary is artificial. We made it up. Or, better stated, our minds made it up.

Why have we done this? Why do we insist on creating a divide between the two? Largely because it is more convenient for our thinking to do so. It is easier to comprehend. Does it make better sense to our rational minds if they are separated? Never mind that these dimensions were never meant to be separated; never mind that they are both part of the human experience; never mind that it is unnatural to subdivide these two parts of our essential beingness. We do it because it appears to make "sense." Yet it doesn't! Look at the world and it's obvious that this boundary is bogus. Still we persist in reinforcing it through adamant attachment to our thoughts, those sacred core beliefs that will surely lead us to extinction unless we take another path, transform our thinking, and reintegrate ourselves into wholeness.

So forget what I said a few paragraphs ago about balancing on one foot. I lied. It is time to stand on both feet!

This stand is what this book is about. It is about awakening latent potentialities in the human race, unleashing our social consciousness as thoughtful and soulful beings. This stand is about ending the lies we tell ourselves, dispelling the myths that keep us prisoners of our circumstances and prevent us from seeking a higher destiny for humankind.

People are stronger together than they are separately. We are also much wiser together. We are at a stage in evolution where we need each other to get past this plateau in our development, where we can break loose and reach our true potential as human beings. Our diversity is our strength. It will allow us to transcend our limitations, both those external to us and those we harbor within. With six-and-a-half billion of us we have a hell of an opportunity! Why bother trying to be like the other person? Let's become fully alive individually, uniquely ourselves at full power, and together create this new possibility.

HUMANITY'S PROMISE

While we claim to admire people and groups who achieve great things —achievements most people think of as impossible—many of us "lead lives of quiet desperation," resigned to taking various anesthetics to make things more tolerable. Record amounts of antidepressants are consumed, and addiction to various substances and behaviors is standard fare. Clearly we have become a society that has renounced its idealism and traded it for lives of busy nothingness. The best available explanation is that we find it too painful to maintain our idealism; the disappointment is too difficult to handle. But we pay a price for renouncing our idealism. We give up a piece of our soul—as people, as nations, and as citizens of the world.

Americans have apparently given up on the dream that gave birth to the United States in the mid-1770s. That idealistic dream which embodied a spiritual core so empowering that our founders formed a brand new country based on a radical new idea for governance—a government by and for the people. An idea untested on such a grand scale.

I find it fascinating that so many historical milestones took place around this time—each a major piece of our nation's founding. Thomas Paine wrote one of the most influential works on this radical idea for American governance in his 1776 booklet *Common Sense*, which remarkably sold 500,000 copies, a number which would rank it as a "blockbuster" bestseller nowadays. In 1775, James Watt perfected his steam engine—an invention that marked the beginning of the Industrial Age. In the very next year, moral philosopher Adam Smith published *The Wealth of Nations*—his famous treatise on free market economics that has since become the "bible of capitalism." In the same time period, the doctrine of the Divine Right of Kings—which had legitimized autocratic dictatorship for much of human history—was coming to an end. All of these milestones occurred on the coattails of what became known as the "Age of Enlightenment" in the eighteenth century.

The age of the machine, modern democracy, free markets, and thinking for ourselves were all significant milestones in humanity's evolution—all converging in historic alignment. Adding to this bundling of significant events, philosopher Immanuel Kant wrote about "daring to know" in his 1784 essay "What Is Enlightenment?"—well after this distinctive period got underway. He identified dogma—or adopted belief, usually accepted teachings of another—as the "ball and chain of man's permanent immaturity."

An emerging new idealism and the death throes of old ideas gave birth to the United States of America. Ideas of legitimated autocracy,

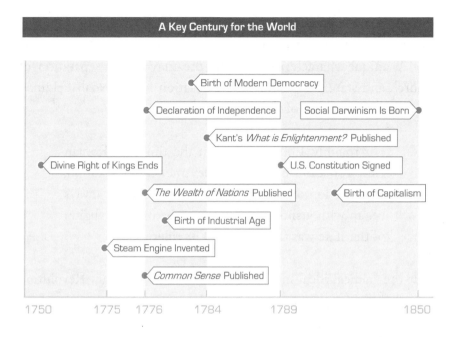

A Key Century for the World

Birth of Modern Democracy

Declaration of Independence

Social Darwinism Is Born

Kant's *What is Enlightenment?* Published

Divine Right of Kings Ends

U.S. Constitution Signed

The Wealth of Nations Published

Birth of Capitalism

Birth of Industrial Age

Steam Engine Invented

Common Sense Published

1750   1775 1776   1784   1789   1850

being told what to think, horse and oxen-power travel and farming, and privileged commerce gave way to democratic governance, thinking for ourselves, free market economics and mechanized power. The Industrial Age, capitalism and modern democracy took life-giving breath as people dared to know and freed their own thinking from some biological back burner, while the tag team of church and state dictated the *wisdom du jour* for the masses. Is it any wonder the very DNA of American culture is comprised of free thinking, entrepreneurial, freedom-loving and technology-driven ideologies when it descended from such a powerful alignment of chromosomes?

The original American Dream was filled with idealism. It represented the dreams of the founding fathers and all their constituents who felt so strongly that they could create an exciting free society.

The dream of the revolutionary generation was derived from the Enlightenment, that our leaders would be "men of merit" who governed only in the public interest and possessed "natural virtue." Thus, as U.S. cultural historian and social critic Morris Berman asserts,

"Love, in effect, would be the social equivalent of gravity, the principle of attraction that would hold everything together."

A unique characteristic of this dream was the separation of church and state. New America Foundation fellow Noah Feldman explains the thinking of the country's founders:

> For roughly 1,400 years, from the time the Roman Empire became Christian to the American Revolution, the question of church and state in the West always began with a simple assumption: the official religion of the state was the religion of its ruler . . .

But the "radical idea" introduced during the American Revolution was that the people were sovereign. He continues:

> This arrangement profoundly disturbed the old model of church and state. To begin with, America was religiously diverse: how could the state establish the religion of the sovereign when the sovereign people in America belonged to many faiths—Congregationalist, Anglican, Presbyterian, Baptist, Quaker. Furthermore, the sovereign people would actively believe in religion instead of cynically manipulating it and elite skeptics would no longer be whispering in the ears of power. Religion would be a genuinely popular, even thriving, political force. This model called for a new understanding of church and state, and the framers of the American Constitution rose to the occasion. They designed a national government that, for the first time in Western history, had no established religion at all.[1]

Founded as a republic based on nondenominational spiritual principles, the United States offered hope to the world. Our founders started a great experiment in human society, based on a philosophy that inspired people worldwide.

The original American Dream was achievable, a vision to which people could commit themselves. It was unprecedentedly bold, a compelling and powerful idea, backed by conviction and deed, and shared by the American patriots who knew they could implement their dream. They dared to know they could achieve their dream, something quite new after centuries of people being told what they should know by "authorities" like the church or the throne.

Nobel Laureate and South African Archbishop Desmond Tutu once stated, "When people decide they want to be free . . . there is nothing that can stop them." The American Dream was so powerful it began attracting people from other nations by the thousands, later by the millions.

WHO ARE WE AND WHAT DO WE WANT?

Some years back, before voicemail, a friend of mine recorded a memorable message on his answering machine. As I recall, it went something like this: "Hi, this is Gary. At the sound of the beep please tell me who you are and what you want. If you think these are trivial questions, be reminded most of us have been trying to figure this out all our lives."

These kinds of questions have been the focus of philosophers, mystics, clergy and teachers of all varieties. Anyone who has embarked upon some level of self-examination, personal development, vision quest, or other inner exploration has most likely ventured into this inquiry as well.

When Apollo 15 astronaut Dave Smith stepped onto the moon in 1971 and proclaimed, "there's a fundamental truth to our nature; man must explore," he was affirming a deep-seated need of human beings. Once we have satisfied our survival needs like food, sex, shelter, relationship and safety, we human beings are compelled to explore the unknown. We have wondered about everything, searched the Earth, are still exploring space (the macro) and the world of sub-atomic particles (the micro). Wherever there is a frontier, a horizon beyond which we cannot see, humans need to check it out. Indeed, we must explore!

We have made huge technological advances in recent years. We have gained widespread wisdom from sages throughout the ages. Yet some of us wonder why we haven't achieved the peaceful and secure existence here on Earth that we claim to want. Who are we and what do we really want?

In the past century we have experienced breakthroughs of all kinds that allow us to create the kind of world we want for ourselves. So it isn't a matter of the conditions being right. We have the wherewithal.

The cynics cry, "It will always be the way it has been." This is a disillusioned perspective, resigned to the present reality being as good as it gets. This is hardly the song of an adventurous human eager to explore the unknown, setting out on the quest for what lies over the horizon. The cynic has lost the spirit of adventure, the spirit of exploration, and, perhaps, the spirit of being human.

Let us reengage that inner explorer in us and leave space to NASA and the other outer-space experts. Let us leave the oceans to the people already engaged in those explorations and leave the study of subatomic particles to the world's scientists. With all these people and organizations fully engaged in their adventures into these un-charted territories, there are still at least five billion of us who could start exploring who we are and what we want.

We have everything we need to pull it off except, perhaps, the will. The first step is to choose. We must decide that the promise of humanity is important enough to stand for it . . . and stand tall for it with all our might. Then we may get closer to answering the question of who we are and start acting more consistently with what we want.

FROM PREDATOR TO COLLABORATOR

Human evolution has taken us from an era when we lived as predators toward a more collaborative way of life. As we solve certain survival issues, we have begun to learn that positive evolution comes with collaboration, so that our first instinct is not to slay someone but instead to engage with them.

We are a far cry from being a society of collaborators, but we certainly are closer than ever, while still possessing some of our predatory instincts. On this continuum—from completely predatory to complete collaboration—we sit midway, with some of us embracing the collaborative approach while others of us maintain our predatory ancestral trait. Our roots may lie in predation, but we possess the ability to transcend them through conscious evolution—an option we human beings possess exclusively. We have the ability to evolve on purpose.

Together we can do what we cannot do separately. Our challenges are beyond the heroic actions of the few. This means that collaboration is essential to make the shift to a new consciousness, a new reality.

GROWING INTO GLOBALISTS

I've always liked what Paine said a few centuries ago. While he identified largely with the United States, he nonetheless saw himself as a global citizen. He stated, "My country is the world. My countrymen are mankind." He writes, "The cause of America is in a great measure the cause of all mankind." He never meant this egocentrically but saw the principles underlying America's Declaration of Independence as ultimately applicable to *all* humanity, addressing issues of importance to people everywhere.

Visionary inventor Buckminster ("Bucky") Fuller saw the whole world as his home and offered a wonderful metaphorical phrase that has stuck with me since the early 1980s. He writes:

In all reality I never "leave home." My backyard has just grown progressively bigger and more globular until now the whole world is my spherical backyard. "Where do you live?" and "What are you?" are progressively less sensible questions. At present I am a passenger on Spaceship Earth and I don't know what I am. I know that I am not a category, a highbred specialization. I am not a thing—a noun. I am not flesh. At eighty-five, I have taken in over a thousand tons of air, food, and water, which temporarily became my flesh and which progressively disassociated from me. You and I seem to be verbs—evolutionary processes. Are we not integral functions of the Universe?[2]

We humans have done very well in developing our abilities to distribute information, travel easily, entertain one another, produce and merchandize our goods and, generally, manage our material reality. However, as great as our material achievements are, we have not kept pace with our internal development.

Somewhere the vision of the founders of the United States got skewed so that the focus came to be only on the material aspects of their dream and not the mystical or spiritual—what Benjamin Franklin called "superintending Providence." Washington saw liberty as obedience to what is highest within ourselves and within the community, not simply having the freedom to pursue selfish interests. But somewhere along the line, the pursuit of happiness started walking on one leg—the leg of materialism—and the spiritual part of the dream, what was referred to as "inner wealth" by the founders, atrophied and we started deferring to structures of doctrine, dogma and interpretations by others rather than exploring our inner selves.

The meaning of the American Dream shifted and became much more about possessions and material abundance. I witnessed this personally when I was growing up in the 1940s and 1950s. Perhaps it was a reaction to the 1929 Stock Market Crash and the Great Depression in which people of my parents' generation suffered so much, but "a chicken in every pot" gave way to "two cars in every garage." Along the way, a big part of the American Dream became owning one's home. It seems we have been measuring our happiness by what we own for several generations now.

Philosopher Jacob Needleman writes, "America is a nation formed by philosophical ideals that have been thought through by human beings—it is the only nation in the world that is so constituted." This country was born from this convergence of ideals amidst a world that was steeped in older ways.

Now is the time for a similar birth—an intentional birth based on a more mature humanity—*but for our entire world*. Now is the time for humanity to take a stand for its greatness—owning a destiny that has been lying dormant on the social level, but still sought by people in their private reflections and deeper yearnings.

The American Dream was meant to be a fresh start. It was unleashed idealism, free to roam in an entirely new country. Now, having run out of "new frontiers," we need to bring the dream home, wherever that may be. Besides, we are too small a world these days. A resurrected American Dream for the exclusive benefit of people in the United States is no longer an option. For better or for worse, the world has become Fuller's Spaceship Earth, and all humans are passengers. One big difference between a spaceship and an airplane: on Spaceship Earth we are also crew members. You can't sit back in your luxury seat, expect to be waited on and remain passive. We each have personal responsibility for how our spaceship does and whether or not we all survive.

Becoming wealthy and powerful as individuals or as nations no longer provides assurance of security or safety. We are all in this together. It is time for a new renaissance in which we bring new commitments and values and approaches to our *world* much like America's founders tried to do over 250 years ago for their *country*.

What the U.S. founders referred to as "one nation, indivisible" can now be paraphrased as "one world, indivisible," consistent with the Spaceship Earth metaphor.

It is time to resurrect the spiritual context for happiness, not continue walking on the one leg of materialism. It is time to explicitly engage that ineffable quality the founders attempted to instill in America's essential DNA—what some of them called "Providence" and others called "Reason." A 2005 article in *Time* magazine focused on Americans' happiness. It reported that "there's evidence of a creeping dissatisfaction too. Why else are so many of us flocking to therapists, consulting divorce lawyers, scarfing Prozac? Why do so many reach middle life with a surprising sense of emptiness? Why does the self-help book remain such a reliable cash machine? In a society as wealthy and privileged as in the U.S., what, after all, does it take to find real satisfaction in life?"

According to research done at the University of Illinois and in The Netherlands, money can only buy happiness up to a point. As *Radical Middle* newsletter reports, "Beyond a certain minimum point, more stuff won't make us happy. Beyond a certain minimum point, you need to go after happiness directly—via family, friends, 'good work'—via whatever gives you a larger sense of purpose and meaning."

Let us come together, in a global community, allowing our innate desire to be connected to catalyze the triumph of the human spirit over the problems and conditions we currently experience. Let us come together as people, not as separate nations or tribes or nationalities but as human beings with a yet-unfulfilled destiny, sharing this experience here on Earth, and cocreate the new dawn for the human spirit. We have so much to learn from one another. The United States can learn much from Europe, Asia and so many others, and vice versa. The Northerners can learn much from the Southern Hemisphere peoples, and vice versa. South Africa has so much to teach us all about reconciling generations of deeply instilled hatred and patterns of violence and vengeance. There's so much more we can all be *together*, as global citizens; so much more than all of us proceeding separately.

THE MATURE HUMAN

You know how teenagers crave their freedom from their parents' control but are less excited about taking responsibility for it? This awkward stage of maturation is where we humans find ourselves right now, on the brink of a *new* enlightenment—a step toward a wiser, more adult human being. Kant writes, "Enlightenment is man's emergence from his self-incurred immaturity." Maturity calls for responsibility to accompany the freedom we can enjoy as adults, not freedom without accountability like so many adolescents seek.

Duane Elgin has worked as a senior social scientist with the think tank SRI International, where he coauthored numerous studies on the long-range future for government agencies such as the National Science Foundation. He has also worked as a senior staff member of the joint Presidential-Congressional Commission on the American Future. In his 2009 book, *The Living Universe*, he describes what this maturing process may look like:

> Eventually we will see that we have an unyielding choice between a badly injured (or even stillborn) species-civilization, and the birth of a bruised, but relatively healthy, human family and biosphere. In seeing and accepting responsibility for this inescapable choice, we will work to discover a common sense of reality, identity, and social purpose.

This is maturity. And, like physical maturing, it may not be easy. Elgin continues:

> Finding this new common sense will be an extremely demanding task. Only after we have exhausted all

hope of partial solutions will we be willing to move forward with an open mind and heart toward a future of mutually supportive development. Ultimately, in moving through our initiation, we will grow from our adolescent ways as a species into our early adulthood and consciously take responsibility for our relationship with the Earth, the rest of life, and the universe.[3]

It is immature to defer to others and let them tell us what to do—a way of avoiding responsibility for our actions and thoughts. Such avoidance happens in groups such as cults where a leader has undue influence over how others think and what commitments they pay lip service to. Our ancestors deferred to the monarchies before the Age of Enlightenment, and as individuals we all did it as children and later as teenagers. There was some comfort in having someone tell us what was right or wrong, what to do or not do. However, taking comfort in this abdication of responsibility as an adult is a cop-out.

Kant writes:

Enlightenment is man's leaving his self-caused immaturity. Immaturity is the incapacity to use one's own understanding without the guidance of another. Such immaturity is self-caused if its cause is not lack of intelligence but lack of determination and courage to use one's intelligence without being guided by another. The motto of enlightenment is therefore: *Sapere aude!* Have courage to use your own intelligence![4]

Futurist Walter Truett Anderson poses a deep and thought-provoking question in his 2003 book *The Next Enlightenment*: "Are we more free than we wish?" Isn't this a challenging question—especially for Americans who claim freedom as their master franchise?

Are we truly afraid of awakening to full liberation and maturity? Much like the frightened teenager who's too proud to admit it, are we facing a historical choice to either grow up or continue living at home under the influence of Mommy and Daddy—being told what to do? Have we fully grown into the maturity of the Age of Enlightenment offered us a couple of centuries ago, or are we still weaning ourselves from the mother's milk of the dictates of church or king—or of Mommy and Daddy?

Like teenagers, who demand independence but know, and secretly value, that they can rely on their parents to cover for them if they get into trouble, are we prone to this sort of fundamentalism—believing what others put forth and avoiding our own innate knowing? Anderson refers to "the shock of recognition" when we first realize that we know what we have been denying we know. When this shock occurs, we can either embrace the knowledge that we do in fact know, or run away from it, scurrying down our underground tunnels pretending we never recognized it to begin with.

This new Age of Enlightenment requires explicit recognition of not only what we've been pretending we don't know, but the full recognition of our spiritual nature—our interconnectedness with a power greater than ourselves. Recognizing these truths is key to becoming mature adults, not only for the population of the United States but for the entire world. Engaging this new stage in human evolution allows us all to transcend the conditions in which we seem so hopelessly stuck.

This recognition requires a new level of maturity, taking responsibility for the whole, being accountable for our choices, individually and collectively. We must grow up!

In the spring of 1996, a few months before he learned he had a fatal cancer, visionary social scientist Willis Harman wrote an article in which he suggested that the constant push for greater productivity and consumption, combined with growing unemployment, was a spiritual crisis rather than an economic one. This certainly goes against the consensus, as matters of employment, GNP and economic growth dominate our culture, our media and our work lives. He writes, "The modern world has more or less equated society with the economy, and contribution with having a job in the mainstream economy." He then challenges the reader to acknowledge that the old ways of job creation and economic production are no longer viable— something any mature, thinking person must see if they look beyond the immediate future. He states the old way "no longer works, and may never again work, may at first seem alarming (or so threatening it is denied). Viewed differently," he offers, "it is a challenge that may induce us to create the good society we all know is possible." [5]

The Great Growing Up is about what Harman calls "the good society we all know is possible," which is certainly an idea whose time has come. I say this boldly because almost everyone knows we can do better.

Here again, we are challenged to acknowledge that we know what's possible. We also know the likely outcome if we continue denying what we know, or pretending that we don't know. Despite how our minds react to this assertion, and how defensive we might get initially, if we take the time to ask ourselves in deep introspection, most of us will cop to it and admit we really do know. We know what is needed, what is wrong, and that there is a possible better future waiting for us if we put our minds to it.

Michael Dowd was trained as a Christian minister yet managed to reconcile the often opposing views of religion and science is his 2009 book, *Thank God for Evolution*. He addresses this "promise of possibility" of historic proportions:

> We are on the verge of the greatest spiritual awakening in history. It took centuries for the Copernican Revolution to transform humanity. Thanks to global satellite telecommunications, the Internet, and all the other technologies that link us, it is quite possible

that our own paradigm shift—from seeing nature as an artifact, to seeing Nature as the primary revelation of divinity (and inseparable from that divinity)—will prevail over the course of decades rather than centuries. That the shift will occur eventually is almost certain. How fast it transforms our institutions depends on how rapidly and thoroughly we are transformed as individuals, and where we choose to invest our collective creativity as awareness expands.[6]

CONSCIOUS EVOLUTION

It is time to stop thinking about what *might* happen in the future and start thinking about what we *want* to happen, about what needs to occur *now* to bring that desired future about. This is "conscious evolution."

Many find this term a kind of oxymoron because evolution is thought of as survival of the fittest, something seemingly left to chance and random circumstances. But as we evolve as human beings we are also growing in consciousness, and, as we do, we have more and more choice in how we evolve. Being conscious of the choice makes evolution self-transcendent. We can either evolve on purpose or by accident. But it is our choice.

Not making a choice is still making a choice. Choosing not to do something, while passive and seemingly inconsequential, is nonetheless a choice. The primary question is: What is our intention? Our intentionality will almost always generate our reality. Forget what we *say* we want; forget what we *think* we want; if you want to see what your intention is, look at what you are *doing*.

So, the conundrum before us is: Do we wish to create a future and have some hand in the kind of world we want, or are we willing to simply accept whatever six billion people passively allow to happen? Are we willing to be cocreators in our growth as a species, or are we resigned to whatever fate awaits us without our proactive participation. Do we prefer "self-transcendent evolution" or "accidental evolution" as we consider the kind of world we will be leaving our children's children?

So many of us have this notion that humans are merely advanced primates, implying we have no further to evolve. Influenced by Darwin and possibly zoologist Desmond Morris's 1967 book *Naked Ape*, we can become trapped in this self-limiting image of ourselves. I invite you to envision that we have a far way to go in human evolution, and that we may never know what the ultimate evolution is or when it will occur, if at all.

Barbara Marx Hubbard, president of the Foundation for Conscious Evolution, examines the potential we have as an entire species to evolve with intention, consciously, and create a future of our own choosing rather than a simple projection of what's happened in our past. She writes:

> In the midst of our confusion, however, a new story of evolution is emerging that has the potential to inspire us to creative action. It is coming from the combined insights of many disciplines: scientific, historical, psychological, ecological, social, spiritual, and futuristic. But it has not yet found its artistic or popular expression. We discover fragments in journals, poems, books, lectures, conferences, seminars, and networks of those interested in it. But it has not yet been pieced together and told with the power required to awaken the social potential within us and to guide us in the 21st century toward a future of infinite possibilities.

Hubbard elaborates further:

> Conscious Evolution is a social movement, a call to action that offers real hope for the world. In fact, it

is a "movement of movements." It connects positive, life-enhancing initiatives and insights in every field leading toward a higher level of cooperative action. It stimulates learning, personal mastery and systems theory applied to social change . . . it brings forth practical visions of hope and the fulfillment of humanity's most profound aspirations.[7]

She sees Conscious Evolution as a new worldview "composed of the growing edge of all disciplines seen as parts of a living whole." This could possibly set the framework for a "meta-religion," she says, meaning an "all-inclusive space in which the great faiths and wisdom traditions can contribute their unique gifts to the conscious evolution of humanity." She considers Conscious Evolution to be the emergence of "a universal humanity" capable of "co-evolution with nature" and "co-creation with Spirit." This is not only choosing to evolve, on purpose, but to do so in alignment with all of the world's spiritual principles and energies.

We are not mere animals. We are not naked apes! We are human beings.

I've heard a term used for our global society beyond this new frontier of conscious evolution: "wisdom society." This implies that a more mature humanity comes forward and ceases leaving our continued evolution to happenstance. It affirms that the human race sets out an intention for a consciously manifested future for us all and that there is enough consciousness on Earth right now to make it happen.

Consciousness is causal. Physical reality reflects our state of mind, our consciousness. We have morphed from an old mindset that could be characterized by "I'll believe it when I see it"—a paradigm with physical reality considered to be the ultimate reality—to a paradigm whose tagline might be "I'll see it when I believe it"—a mindset in which our consciousness determines our reality. Consciousness is the next frontier for human evolution, much like "daring to know" was the next frontier when the Divine Right of Kings was the prevailing mindset in the world.

The only thing keeping us in the reality we endure is the consciousness we are choosing at the present time. Reality changes as our consciousness changes.

Evolving on purpose, or conscious evolution, is an adult choice, made by a mature population that is engaged in its own development, taking responsibility for choosing its own future. We have the power to either eradicate ourselves or take the leap. It is really a choice.

Australian government policy advisor John Stewart writes in his book *Evolution's Arrow* that when people "decide to continue to serve the dictates of past evolution they are choosing evolutionary failure, in the full knowledge that they are doing so." They are "choosing a life that is meaningless, absurd and ridiculous from an evolutionary perspective, and know that they are making such a choice." Harsh words for our fellow human beings!

If, however, people want to contribute "to the formation of a cooperative and evolvable planetary society that manages the matter, energy and living processes of the planet" to form organizations of a larger scale and greater "evolvability," Stewart says their actions will contribute to "the next great step in the evolution of life on earth."

Mystics, poets, songwriters and philosophers address matters of meaning, longing and other human but intangible yearnings behind the passions that help us wake up every day, motivate us to get out of bed, move us to stand for something. These are those meaningful things that motivate us to be good parents, great performers, reliable workers, faithful partners and, in general, a unique species that wants to explore and expand into something beyond our awareness, even if it is unexplainable or ineffable. In other words, there is always a "new" frontier for us.

The "American experiment" can serve the world because the U.S. is a microcosm of Earth. It has the most diverse population, in some cases having ethnic communities almost as large—sometimes larger—as those in their homelands. All religions, races, national origins and ethnicities make America their home. The U.S. is also the first nation to be founded on the principle that people deserve to be free to find their own happiness, in whatever form that takes.

Americans have wrestled with the challenges of implementing the original American Dream, which included straying from its original intent and spirit—violating, then defending, the principles under which we were founded and squabbling over our differences. We have fought each other in a civil war, shouted across the aisle at each other in Congress, killed one another over silly differences, and have become the world's most arrogant, obscene and conspicuous consumers in the world. But, despite all these faults, we remain united—one nation, glaringly transparent.

The Great Dream can be an extension of the original American Dream if the world can embrace it as everybody's dream, humanity's dream. Is this a challenge? You bet! Hey, we in the United States are still learning and growing, finding our way along this difficult path to our original vision. We keep getting lost, then find our way back, and then we wander off that path again. But we love challenges. We've proven that over our short history. Life without challenges can be pretty boring, so let's expand the vision and embrace the challenges even if this means we have to change, grow and evolve to have the dream.

Bucky Fuller foresaw the potential for humanity through the eyes of the visionary scientist and inventor. Upon the birth of his daughter, he took stock of his life from a different point of view, that of a parent. While he had not achieved financial wealth, he did realize that he possessed a "rich inventory of experience" and chose to change himself in a profoundly deep way. He writes:

> That experience made clear to me that there were critical problems to be solved regarding total humanity

aboard planet Earth—problems that would take at least a half-century to cope with successfully; problems as yet unattended to by anyone; problems that, if successfully solved, would bring lasting advantage to all humanity; problems that, if left unsolved, would find all humanity at ever-increasing disadvantage.

It was not that the problems could not be seen by others, but society was preoccupied with individual, national, state, and local business-survival problems, which forced its leaders into short-term, limited-scope considerations—with no time for total world problems. The presidents of great corporations had to make good profits within a very few years or lose their jobs. The politicians, too, were preoccupied with short-range national, state, or municipal survival matters.

Bucky saw that the world was in a trance of sorts, entranced by a self-convincing ideology that humans are the fittest to survive despite their stupidity.

What my experience taught me was that if the physical laws thus far found by science to be governing Universe were intelligently and fearlessly employed in the production of ever higher performances per each pound of material, erg of energy, and second of time invested, it would be feasible to take care of all humanity at higher standards of living than had ever been known by any humans—and to do so sustainingly.[8]

From 1927 until the end of his life in 1983, Bucky dedicated himself to this end.

Paul Ehrlich, preeminent Stanford biologist and author of *The Population Bomb*, wrote a book entitled *The Dominant Animal* with his wife Anne in 2008. They look at humankind's prospects for the future:

> The world in general seems to be gradually awakening to a realization that our long evolutionary story is, through our actions but not our intentions, coming to a turning point. A product of evolution ourselves, shaped by the environments of our past, we have attained dominance by increasing our numbers, diverting resources, and reshaping the world's environments to sustain our huge, still growing population. That dominance has now led to a progressive destabilization of the global systems that sustain us.

They close the book with this:

> Humanity's globalizing civilization must take this enhanced opportunity to exploit conscious evolution and try new ways of organizing societies to cooperate to solve its burgeoning global problems . . . each day that we do nothing forecloses options for creating a better future for ourselves and our fellow inhabitants of earth. The qualities that made it possible for us to become the dominant animal could now be put to use in creating a sustainable future for ourselves and the rest of the living world.[9]

Chapter 2

OUR PRESENT REALITY

What motivated America's founders, many of whom had been prosperous and had no need to risk their fortunes and their families' security? Why did they feel the need to risk their fortunes and their lives as well? What was the spark that lit fires in the bellies of those men and women who risked so much for this American Dream?

Here we are, two-and-a-half centuries later and, once again, we have allowed ourselves to be subordinated. But, unlike in the days of the American colonists, the enemy isn't some far- reaching empire. The enemy is us.

One aspect of this part of our nature as human beings is addressed in the 2007 bestselling book *The Black Swan*, by Nassim Nicholas Taleb. The "black swan" is the author's name for an unforeseen event. In discussing all the ways we tend to delude ourselves he writes:

> The problem is our ideas are sticky; once we produce a theory, we are not likely to change our minds—so those who delay developing their theories are better off . . . there is a tendency not to reverse opinions we already have. Remember that we treat ideas like possessions, and it will be hard for us to part with them.[1]

We can speak the truth now and acknowledge the new lie: *the prospects for a better world depend upon continuous growth and channeling resources through the king of our hubris or ego.* Let us resign from this imperialist tyrant and remove ourselves from being under the monarchy we have legitimized, the system we installed as a replacement for the King of England. And let us start by debunking some of the many myths we have come to accept as truth.

DEBUNKING OLD MYTHS

In the upcoming pages we will examine many commonly understood "facts" or myths as they are popularly understood. As we will see, many are simply popular ideas that underpin our perception of reality. Might we need to question more of the underlying assumptions on which our beliefs are based? You decide. Here are a few that seem to have attracted some significant legitimacy over the years:

1. *There needs to be a majority of people to make big changes happen.* In fact, rarely is change brought about by large numbers of people. Almost always, large scale changes are caused by smaller groups of people who feel passionately about their cause. To quote anthropologist Margaret Mead, "Never doubt that a small group of thoughtful, committed citizens can change the world. Indeed, it is the only thing that ever has."

2. *Physical matter is all that is real, the "stuff" of life; abstractions are not for pragmatists.* While this used to be the belief of empirical science, quantum physics has shown this was inaccurate and that fields of energy which cannot be seen are incredibly "real."

3. *To get change to happen we need better or different designated leaders.* Leaders who are elected or appointed often follow the lead of their supporters: they respond to the pressure rising from their backers and get into sync with it. As former U.S. Ambassador to NATO Harlan Cleveland writes, "Those

with visible responsibility for leadership are nearly always too visible to take responsibility for change."[2]

4. *Evolution is something that happens over millions of years; there's nothing I can do to influence it.* Evolution is happening much faster than most people realize. Evolution is exponential; change is happening with greater and greater speed. We now have the ability to "go extinct" in seconds, learn anything known to the human mind in mere minutes, reach almost anyone in the world in a few hours, travel around the world or change our sex in a matter of days, and start a company in a week. A quick look at the developments of the past half-century can convince all but the most adamant myth-holder of this misperception.

5. *Our scarcest assets are the Earth's natural resources.* Our scarcest resources are not water or oil, as people might think. The thing we have the least of and need the most is human attention.

6. *Nature is a place we go to visit, to vacation or renew or relax.* This implies that we are separate from Nature. We are as much a part of Nature as the fish, the eagle and the wolf. Our habitats are just as much a part of Nature as the eagle's nest, termite hills or beavers' dams.

7. *I can count on the media to get all the news that's really important.* All the media provides is scant coverage of a few headlines, usually involving controversy, trials, disasters or scandals. Most of what is reported is opinion, gossip and speculation— none of which is very meaningful.

8. *We are smarter than any of the previous generations in history.* Quantum physics and the growing appreciation for ancient wisdom strongly suggest that we may be the best informed but not necessarily the wisest generations of human beings. Every day we learn of new wisdom from indigenous cultures we once considered "primitive."

9. *Everyone wants a better world.* While we are quick to assume every human being is motivated by self-preservation and wants to improve the human condition, there are some people who are heavily invested in having the world end, or in *their* world ending, including those who are waiting for the apocalypse and those killing and dying for jihad.

10. *If only poorer countries could develop economically they'd be fine.* Economic development without human development is a waste of money; it is a myth perpetuated by the elite and often by patronizing nations who do not understand the cultures of the developing world. Therefore, billions of development funds are frequently wasted and situations are often made worse.

11. *Paradoxes must be reconciled.* This is an outmoded idea, mostly perpetuated by men, many of whom cannot tolerate ambiguity and seeming contradictory opposites coexisting. Women have less difficulty accepting this reality, which exists throughout Nature. Insisting that all paradox must be resolved requires unnatural and inaccurate labels, often resulting in the creation of a false truth for the sake of maintaining this intolerance.

12. *Really big change takes lots of time.* While we rarely know every facet of what contributes to large-scale social change, we have seen it occur seemingly almost overnight. While many forces may have been at play in less than obvious ways for an extended period of time, paradigms can change quite suddenly (and often do).

13. *Large-scale change takes lots of money and lots of people to make it happen.* Changing the way we think requires no change in fiscal policies, no budget, no new laws. And we know this change is already underway, and it has, and can, only grow from the people, truly grassroots.

14. *A panel of experts is the best way to get the smartest decisions.* Designated experts frequently will come up with less wise

solutions than a diverse mix of experts and nonexperts (see: *The Wisdom of Crowds* by James Surowiecki cited later).

15. *I know the world needs to change but I don't know what to do.* This is total bull! It is the lie we keep telling ourselves in order to feel better about not doing anything to make the world better. Collectively we possess enough wisdom to take care of every problem in the world and make just about anything happen.

16. *Humans have always had wars and always will.* This is inherently false but is the cherished motto of the cynic and the fatalist. There are no reasons for wars to be predestined conclusions other than the legitimacy we humans give to the idea that war is inevitable. Conflict can and has been resolved without resorting to armed conflict.

17. *Gross Domestic Product (GDP) is a good thing; it measures how healthy we are economically as a nation.* This is deceptive because GDP can rise and only a few people can be doing better while the masses might be doing much worse. GDP measures monies spent on building more prisons, hiring more police or military, increased healthcare costs due to toxins and pollution, and other expenses that not only do not reflect an improvement in the quality of life but could actually reflect a deterioration. In 2004, the Redefining Progress Foundation reported that GDP overestimated the health of the U.S. economy by $7 trillion because of this distortion. The Foundation offered an alternative: Genuine Progress Indicator or GPI updates, which consider both the quality and distribution of economic growth.

18. *Science tells us that we are all separate selves.* New science tells us the opposite! According to *The 2007 Shift Report*: "Science is telling us that we live in a highly dynamic, interactive, interconnected world that is full of potential . . . This interconnectivity means that from a certain perspective

we are not really separate from one another, even though our senses trick us into believing we are. Since our actions and thoughts have such potential to impact one another, we can no longer afford to act out of this illusion of separateness."

19. *Our leaders won't let things get too bad; they know best so I'll leave the big problems to them.* This is archaic thinking, more appropriate to the seventeenth century when serfs deferred to kings. This disguised apathy has no place in the modern world.

20. *There is only so much wealth in the world so for some to have it others must be precluded from having it.* This zero-sum attitude about wealth and money was based on a property-based model where there was a finite amount of land. If one person owned all the land, then others were unable to. This thinking is now outmoded since wealth is now also based on productivity, goodwill and nonland assets which are expandable.

21. *The leadership gap requires more content (trainings, books, workshops, etc.).* There is mounting evidence that more training, books and other content on leadership is not the problem in our lack of leaders. It is lack of implementing what we already know. There is plenty of wisdom already available if people in leadership roles would only apply it.

22. *The more we work, the more we get done.* While this may have been true in the eras of manual labor, it is a complete myth in the modern workplace that requires creativity and fresh ideas. As reported in *Worthwhile* magazine, "American workers generate the same output per hour as their French counterparts—whose working year is 20 percent shorter." Despite the evidence that overwork doesn't produce a pro rata benefit, people are still considered "slackers" in the U.S. if they work only forty-hour work weeks.

23. *The "free market" will guide civilization intelligently.* This core dogma of market capitalism might not be a myth if the

marketplace were truly free. Social Darwinism provides the backdrop for manipulative advertising, government-backed advantages, and clever financial concoctions. These skew the markets so truly free choice is more illusionary than most people believe.

24. *Mergers and acquisitions create value for stockholders, employees and the community.* In his paper "Whole-System Integration," Professor Mel Toomey noted that *Fortune* magazine studied ten acquisitions and found that none measured up to the median return on investment (ROI) and only two made it through the ten-year period without significant difficulty; five of the ten realized negative returns. According to Toomey, New York University reported that in two-thirds of 168 cases investigated, stockholder value fell after mergers and acquisitions (M&A) activity. Tax and accounting giant Deloitte & Touche, LLP, said that one out of two mergers fails because of inadequate planning and poor management. Investments bankers and others involved in "doing the deal" usually make lots of money on M&A transactions, but everyone invested for the long term (career employees, the community, long-term stockholders) usually ends up losing. Seventy to 80 percent of M&As do not produce the business results that were intended! Yet we allow M&A to continue without objection. Seem insane?

25. *The modern corporate system serves free market capitalism.* Wrong! Over the last few centuries there have been several modifications to corporate law that allow for corporations to control our democracy, instead of the way our founders originally intended it—that democracy ("We the People") would have a say in how corporations operated.

These are just twenty-five of the myths many of us live with at home and at work. Do you recognize any of these myths operational in your life and work? Now let us examine our social systems and how well they function today.

SIGNS OF SYSTEMS DYSFUNCTION

There is plenty of evidence that many crises exist at this stage of human evolution. With crisis comes opportunity. But in order to take advantage of the opportunity we need to recognize the crises so we have a decent shot at transcending them. Denying the way things are and how they are going will only cause us to slide further down the slope to disaster, and not convert the crises to opportunities.

One of the advantages of the 2008 financial meltdown is that vastly greater numbers of people have become more aware of our dysfunctional social systems and how much impact they can have globally. Climate change had been getting many people's attention, but some boohooed that or stubbornly argued its inaccuracies. Many held it as remote, beyond affecting them or their families in the near term. But the economy directly affects almost everyone to some degree. Many capitalist countries that used to think of the U.S. as the nation that knows how to make money were jolted into the realization that the "American way" of making large amounts of money is flawed. So, thanks to those Wall Street financial engineers and salespeople, more of us may be open to looking more closely at the systems we have created, and to confirming their functionality in today's world.

Belgian banker Bernard Lietaer writes, "[W]e have now entered the period of an unprecedented convergence of the four planetary issues—financial instability, climate change, unemployment and the financial consequences of an aging society."[3] A handful of people recognized this convergence before September 2008. I suspect far more are looking at these issues with increasing concern now, and thus there might exist a greater receptivity for examining our options and choices toward moving forward.

I often challenge my audiences to point to one social system that is working as intended. I point to the economic system, which some have defended in the past but would find far more difficult and un-popular to do now. Whether it is economics, education, health, politics, media, military, justice—all the systems we've come to depend on as modern human beings—they are all in breakdown or close to it at this time. One sign of these breakdowns is that they are all negatively impacting the natural environment on which we depend for life support.

But here are a few examples of other systems in dysfunction:

Widening Wealth Gap

The world's wealth gap is widening each day. This is a ticking time bomb that will eventually explode with devastating results. The graph below indicates the enormity of this disparity as we perpetuate the continuing trend.

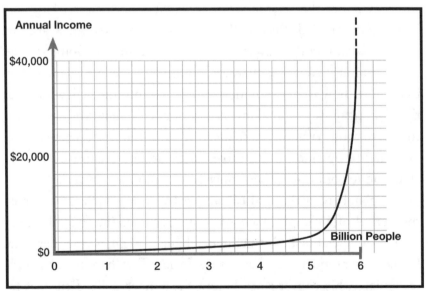

Graph of world income in 2003 from Poke, UK, based on the Global Rich List at http://www.globalrichlist.com/how.html; graph is based upon the following sources: 1. 2003 world population Data Sheet of the Population Reference Bureau; 2. Steven Mosher, president of the Population Research Institute, CNN, October 13, 1999; 3. Branco Milanovic, "True World Income Distribution, 1988 and 1993: First calculations based on household surveys alone," World Bank Development Research Group, November 2000, p.30. *Used with permission.*

Failing War on Drugs

Another of the most obvious examples of systems that don't work is the U.S. is the "War on Drugs." Huge amounts of money, military might and people are allocated to searching out and destroying secret farms and distribution centers in Columbia, Venezuela, and elsewhere, while the primary customers are U.S. citizens. This is akin to the parents of a teenage addict hiring a local militia to destroy the neighborhood drug pusher's supply of drugs and contacts instead of getting their kid to a rehab center so he or she can recover from their addiction. Why do we go after the suppliers when our own people are the customers? Doesn't that seem a bit insane? No wonder the modern War on Drugs has been going on since 1971, at an estimated cost of $50 billion a year, with about one-third of the 1.7 million people being held in U.S. prisons being drug-law offenders. Yet we have made no dent in the traffic coming into the U.S.! Why not focus energies on why U.S. citizens feel such a need to consume illegal drugs, creating a huge market for enterprising international drug cartels to exploit.

My assessment of the War on Drugs does not mean I disrespect all the dedicated work being done by well-meaning and talented people who are engaged in this war. Objectors to wars have often been criticized for this in the past. One can criticize a system's performance or even its efficacy without implying that the people involved are either incompetent or undedicated. In fact, this was the first thing I learned about systems dynamics in the early 1980s. When good-hearted people who are normally effective and competent workers continue to produce a substandard result, or even make the problem worse, you have a pretty good clue the problem isn't personnel but rather systemic.

Losing the War on Cancer

Since 1971, the U.S. has been fighting another war—the War on Cancer. Are we winning? Have we made progress in almost forty years of research and billions of dollars of government and publicly donated funds? According to the Cancer Prevention Coalition (CPC), we are not. They state that from 1973 to 1999 "the overall incidence of cancers . . . has increased by 24%" and conclude that "we are losing the winnable war against cancer."[4] The CPC cites "special interests" as the chief culprit in what it calls a "travesty," despite "well-intentioned" legislation that "displaces control of cancer policy from the public to the private sector." It also accuses the American Cancer Society of being "more interested in accumulating wealth than saving lives." A group of sixty-eight leading national experts in cancer prevention and public health and past directors of three federal agencies expressed their concerns in 1992 by identifying the "escalating incidence of cancer to epidemic proportions over recent decades" as evidence of the war's failure. What's worse, they claimed, the National Cancer Institute and the American Cancer Society mislead and confuse the public by "repeated claims that we are winning the war against cancer." One startling revelation about suspected but unexamined causes: The CPC report claims prescription drugs "may pose higher cancer risks than most other recognized carcinogens." This points again to the problem of special interests, such as drug manufacturers, exercising influence on the outcomes and thus making the war unwinnable.

Growing Lack of Engagement

The *Gallup Management Journal* surveyed U.S. employees in 2006 and discovered that only "31 percent of respondents claimed to be engaged at work, 52 percent were not engaged and 17 percent were 'actively disengaged.'"[5] For a country losing so many jobs to developing nations this trend is potentially disastrous to the world's largest national economy.

MIT professor Peter Senge, one of the patriarchs of systems thinking and system dynamics, says, "The Western model itself is basically bankrupt. It does not give enough attention to the human side of development. It's really very weak . . . and the industrial consumer oriented development has made things very much worse." What is his recommended remedy? He says "service to a much richer concept of development is what is needed."[6] This requires completely different thinking from the convention in the industrialized West, however.

Economism

One of the most glaring signs that something has to change, an attitude that almost everyone in industrialized countries subscribes to and those in developing countries are learning, is the absolute dominance of economics in decision making, to the near exclusion of all other considerations. This has been called "economism" by some economists, meaning the reduction of all social benefits and values to economics. Chris Thomson, former economist and now Director of the School of Consciousness in Spain, describes it thus:

> Economism is the tendency to view the world through the lens of economics, to regard a country as an economy rather than as a society, and to believe that economic considerations and values rank higher than other ones . . . a very narrow way of seeing the world . . . prevents us from seeing whether we are making genuine progress. We assume that if there is more money and economic activity (economic growth), things are getting better. In reality, they might be getting worse and our devotion to economic growth and things economic is probably one of the main reasons for this.[7]

Most of our global problems, such as environment, poverty and education, are exacerbated by decisions based on cost. The least expensive process is frequently chosen over the most environmentally friendly, which also adds pressure to the poverty gap and, thus, to the education gap. The emphasis on financial cost is followed by an emphasis on convenience.

Before we move on from this conundrum, let me address a key factor in the solution—systems thinking. Obviously there is much scholarship on the subject, a field of study and practice that began in the late 1940s. Still a relatively new discipline, much has been published about systems theory, and there is much to learn before we can start thinking from this different set of assumptions—a whole other viewpoint from the one previously held throughout our lives. I strongly recommend that you join me in becoming a perpetual scholar on the subject so we can think naturally and spontaneously from a systems perspective. I promise you will never lose the ability to think linearly, which will still have its uses and practical applications. But we will all be able to deal with complexity in a more competent, effective and leveraged way.

Let us look at why we have so much systems dysfunction going on in our world, and explore possible cultural contributors to this phenomenon.

CULTURE OF FEAR AND SEPARATION

University of Kent professor of sociology Frank Furedi writes:

> Throughout history human beings have had to deal with the emotion of fear. But the way we fear and what we fear changes all the time. During the past 2,000 years we mainly feared supernatural forces. In medieval times volcanic eruptions and solar eclipses were a special focus of fear since they were interpreted as symptoms of divine retribution. In Victorian times many people's fears were focused on unemployment. Today, however, we appear to fear just about everything.[8]

When fear is rampant, strange things happen, usually not good things. Fear draws out the worst in human behavior. As one of America's founders and former U.S. president Thomas Jefferson wrote, "It is not power that corrupts, but fear. Fear of losing power corrupts those who wield it, and fear of the scourge of power corrupts those who are subject to it." The culture of fear we find ourselves in is dominating our choices and our world.

Fear is a natural human emotion that serves a valuable purpose when real danger is imminent. It heightens the senses, puts the body on alert and comes in very handy in dangerous situations. Living in a culture that is permeated with fear, mostly *imagined* fear or worry, as so many live today, is very unhealthy and unnatural. This is also a spiritual crisis. When we live in fear we feel separate, alone and protective. We contract, pulling ourselves inside, and often isolate. When we are afraid, we are often not at our best as people. When we are afraid, we withhold ourselves from the rest of the world—we withhold ourselves *from* the world by isolating and withholding *for* ourselves through selfishness.

When we live in fear we seek control. Life seems safer if we seem to have control. If we cannot have control, we might settle for protecting ourselves. In either case, controlling or protecting, we are kept very busy and separate from others. Have you noticed how busy so many people in the West have become in recent decades? How self-obsessed Americans seem to be? It is almost as if the more we fear, the busier we make ourselves. Perhaps this is because we have much to do in order to mask our fear, or distract ourselves from it. Regardless, this fear occupies much of our attention and our time.

Social scientist Duane Elgin has this to say:

> In moving from a long axial age of separation to one
> of communion and community, a new architecture
> of life will emerge that will weave our everyday lives
> into a larger whole. In a shift similar to that which

nature makes—for example, in the jump from simple atoms to complex molecules, or from complex molecules to living cells—humanity is being challenged to make a jump to a new level of community ... for tens of thousands of years, humanity has been on a path of separation—pulling back from nature and growing our sense of differentiation and empowerment as a species. Now our powers have become so great that they threaten the integrity of life on this planet and confront us with an unprecedented test of our species character. If we move through this time of initiation successfully, we can make our journey of return back into a harmonious relationship with the Earth and the universe that is our original home.[9]

In addressing the issue of fear and separation as a spiritual crisis, *A Course of Love* states:

The world does not keep you separate. You keep yourself separate from the world. This is what made the world the world it is ... The separated self is so ensconced in fear that the known fears of its existence seem preferable to the unknown fears of any other kind of existence. That an option could be chosen that leaves no room for fear at all does not occur to it, for the absence of fear is something it has never known.[10]

In his scholastic treatise on the philosophy of Empedocles, Peter Kingsley writes:

[I]t's only when we realize we are not separate at all that we start to become free ... We are under

a cosmic obligation to become conscious . . . we are
bound to do whatever we can to become more conscious . . . Even the longing to become free, to grow
in awareness, be more conscious, is predetermined by
our inner nature; is our own divine self drawing us to
itself. And to become one at last with that inner nature is to realize everything is bound by absolute laws.
Then we are free: free from the illusion of having to
choose, free simply to be ourselves.[11]

This "separated self" is the ego or unfettered mind, godless self-
will. This is how we separate ourselves from the rest of the world,
perpetuating the myth that we are not connected as human beings.
Separation causes conflict, me being a separate self from you. Arab
and Jew, Christian and Muslim, blacks and whites, men and women,
rich and poor, Protestant and Catholic.

Specialness is a form of withholding oneself. Unfortunately, this
form of indulgence in the separated self is almost always at someone else's expense. Bob Fuller, an advocate for "dignitarian culture"
(a phrase coined by Buckminster Fuller), refers to "rankism" as the
source of all discriminations. Specialness could be a primary cause
of rankism.

Investment banker and journalist David Batstone writes about a
time when he was being interviewed:

I . . . told the journalist that we are living in a culture
of fear. Fear has become as pervasive a cultural moti-
vator as greed, frankly. It goes beyond politics. It goes
beyond marketing and advertising. All of the forego-
ing accept and even manipulate fear, of course. But
at root fear is embedded in the way that we commu-
nicate with each other. We talk with each other assuming that we know how the other person is feeling,

and react out of our own fears as much as their actual disposition.[12]

Fear generates the need to be protective, to hoard what one has acquired. Fear breeds scarcity and furthers the separated state of the ego. Fear leads to the need to control and mistrust anything or anyone we don't have control over. In this state we make what we think of as "free choices," but they are really options we have created based on the culture of fear in which we live.

The culture of fear is so widespread internationally that it may be difficult to observe, since it has been a background conversation impacting how we have constructed our reality for so long. It runs deep and influences almost every decision we make. Unless we transcend this context of fear and create a culture of connection—even the love that America's founders may have had in mind—the picture doesn't look very promising. Berman has a less than optimistic view of what's in store for the U.S.:

> So "terrorism" now replaces communism as the enemy, since this involves only a change of content, not of form, and we are now set to rerun the old scenario at higher stakes—that is, at a rather precarious point in our history. This will mean vastly exaggerating the threat, never looking within ourselves or at our role in the overall scheme of things, persecuting many people at home and probably killing huge numbers abroad, living in an illusion, and in general doing ourselves irreparable harm.[13]

When one's life context is fear and separation, one tends to sometimes act desperately and seek refuge in distraction, addiction and consumption. People seek coping mechanisms rather than experiencing fear directly. They mask their fear behind cynicism and resignation. Mistrust is widespread and anxiety rules. Vacations or holidays are another way we seek refuge from these seemingly unavoidable experiences. In circumstances involving drugs or alcohol, they might be "chemical holidays." These refuges might give temporary comfort or solace, but the effects wear off soon, so we go back for more. The aim is to make life more tolerable for oneself.

Fear generates mistrust, another widespread phenomenon throughout global society. It has infected diplomacy, politics, business, even healthcare. Let's look at U.S. professions and see how they rate for "trustworthiness."

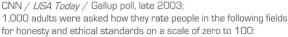

CNN / *USA Today* / Gallup poll, late 2003;
1,000 adults were asked how they rate people in the following fields for honesty and ethical standards on a scale of zero to 100:

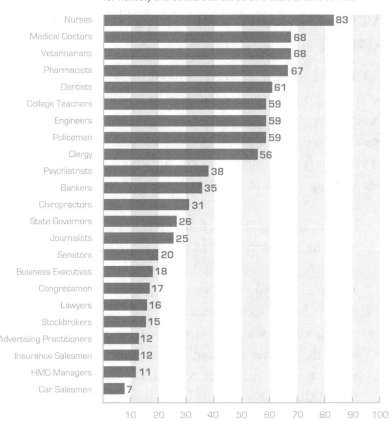

Excerpted from *Worthwhile* magazine, Premier Issue 2004

Ranking the professions we trust or mistrust has become part of our culture, like drawing up the "Best Dressed" list in fashion. But isn't it pathetic that we have such little trust for people upon whom we depend for so much? We trust our sons and daughters to military service when the people who decide if they are going to be "in harm's way" are only trusted one-sixth or one-seventh as much as nurses. We rely on lawyers to keep us safe in legal matters, yet we trust them one-fifth as much as pharmacists. Our health care systems are run by people who are near or at the bottom of the trust ladder, yet we hand over our well-being to them.

Separated self and fear complement one another. They are each invested in having the other in the picture.

COMPLACENT, COMPLIANT AND, THEREFORE, COMPLICIT

Tom Atlee is a pioneer in "societal intelligence." His social change vision is based on new understandings of wholeness that recognize the value of diversity, unity, relationship, context, uniqueness and the spirit inside each of us and the world. This is a systemic approach to social change. Atlee addresses both human evolution and systems change when he writes in a personal e-mail in 2006:

> I knew that solving each of these problems would not solve our propensity to create more problems. To overcome our biological limitations as individuals, we have co-evolved collective systems and capacities—cultural, social, economic, political, scientific, media, educational, public relations, etc. But the flaw in all that is that we have designed them primarily for comfort, profit, power, control, and entertainment rather than for collective intelligence, sanity, and wisdom.[14]

Our organizations, as with all the systems we've created, are outmoded designs for the future we could have. New designs are being called for, yet most of us stick with the old models that keep the status quo in place.

A word about comfort: While many people seek comfort, transitions are almost always uncomfortable. Discomfort is a natural part of life and should not be avoided at the expense of creating something good.

To begin dispelling the popular myths and curing dysfunction in society's systems, we must first tell the truth. This may hurt some feelings and even threaten some institutions that have survived, even thrived, by riding the coattails of the myths they have helped to perpetuate. But the possibility of hurting a few people's feelings is hardly worth society enduring these myths and living in these lies ad nauseam. This requires us to wake up from our doldrums and rejuvenate our aliveness.

Through much of our history we were pretty darn good for what we knew and had available to us at the time. We humans have made great strides in progressing to a life of material prosperity, comfort and intellectual prowess. Whether we are pro or con regarding our present stage of evolution, we have to admit that we've come a long way. It would be sophomoric, however, to assume that we are fully evolved, that we have reached our pinnacle. We are still adolescent in many ways, and one way it shows up is in the simple-mindedness we exhibit in addressing the messes we've made. Like teenagers, we're oversimplifying what it takes to clean up after ourselves. As a friend said recently, it's like we've had this huge keg party that has lasted all weekend. Now it's time to sober up, clean up, and get back to class or work. This requires more adult behavior and thinking. We are growing up, and this acting like adults may be hard to confront. It's far easier for the adolescent to move down the street hoping someone else will clean things up so they can continue to party. This is where we must own our complicity in creating the conditions in which we now live. We enjoy the benefits of all the good, and can hold ourselves proud of our accomplishments. But there has been a penalty for all this growth. There are some negative consequences that have to be faced along with all the positive ones.

Maturity cries out for massive self-reflection as a species. Let us slow the race to the finish enough to pull in for a pit stop and tend to our basic infrastructure as human beings with needs beyond the tangible external, the merely material. Let us insert some mature sanity, sustainability and wisdom before reentering the race. My dream for this book is that it will provide that respite, a place for reflection—not withdrawal, but retreat and renewal.

ADOLESCENT CULTURES

According to James Hollis, Ph.D., Executive Director of the Jung Educational Center of Houston from 1997-2008:

> The characteristics of an adolescent culture are: poor impulse control, short term memory and ignorance of history, addiction to novelty and new sensations, addiction to escalating intensity of sensation, susceptibility to the lethargic summons of drugs and intoxicants, susceptibility to the seduction of gurus, people in power, and authority, and mostly flight from independence and responsibility.[15]

Chapter 3
THE POWER OF CONSCIOUSNESS

One of the major benefits of retreats is they offer an opportunity to do some soul-searching. Without the occasional retreat, we get caught up in obsessions, habits and routines that often put us in a trance of sorts, and we lose touch with life, meaning and purpose. Retreats, particularly when there's a lot of silence for reflection, provide an opportunity to explore the power of our consciousness, the incredible influence our thinking has on the reality in which we live. As stated earlier, consciousness is causal, so it warrants periodic examination.

Looking at all the dysfunction, delusion and myths we've touched on in the previous pages, let us embrace the truth—that *we know*—and stop the pretense. As Paine told us, "We have the power to start the world over again." Indigenous shamans teach that "the world is as you dream it."

As we noted in the introduction in stating the conclusions of the Millennium Project, there is plenty to be hopeful about. However, some might insist there isn't anything to be done.

Notice if you have already made a judgment as to the possibility for such a transformation. See if your own cynicism has been triggered or if some deep-seated skepticism may reside deep within you.

Remember the saying "If you scratch the surface of a cynic you'll find a disillusioned idealist underneath."

Where has our idealism gone? Many of us started off in life full of imagination and wonder-filled ideals. Then painful encounters with what we might label "reality" caused us to retract our idealism as a protective measure and join in with the masses who take solace in some degree of cynicism which masks their past disillusionments and disappointments and seems to make them more endurable. Now we call ourselves "realists" and tell ourselves we've "grown up." We say things like, "Now I see the world as it really is, not how I'd like it to be." With these decisions we have sentenced ourselves to a lifetime of resignation—lives of limited possibility, what Thoreau called "lives of quiet desperation."

Cynicism is a mental construct—a device created by the mind—intended to protect us from additional disappointment and hurt. However, it results in anesthetizing us from our true emotions—like love, desire and passion—that make life worth living.

True visionaries refuse the false comfort of these anesthetics to numb the pain of earlier disappointments. Visionaries maintain their idealism even though it might mean experiencing some heart-wrenching shortfalls or outright failures from time to time. They are undaunted and continue to pursue their visions—filled with unadulterated idealism. They refuse to commit "cynicide"—soul death by cynicism—and suffocate their idealism. While they may drink from the bottle of cynicism on occasion to salve temporary despairs, they soon rally to sobriety and fully reengage their dreams.

To paraphrase nineteenth-century Spanish philosopher José Ortega y Gasset, the cynic is "a parasite of civilization" and lives by denying his or her cynicism. At the same time, one cannot be disappointed if one subscribes to the cynical view. Cynicism cannot fail if all you want to do is avoid the pain of disappointment and be righteous. But it comes with a heavy price. You will be partially dead inside, unable to muster much passion for anything.

We have far too many cynics in our world today. We need more visionaries. So let's try to scratch through any surface of disillusionment, dear reader, and see if we can find the visionary idealist who has been buried all these years. Rather than engage in idealism as fantasy, let's engage idealism as pragmatists and be practical idealists.

THE POWER OF THOUGHT

Polaroid inventor Dr. Edwin Land said, "If you want to generate new ideas, you probably need to stop holding onto old ideas." H.G. Wells tells us, "It is possible to believe all the past is but the beginning of a beginning, and all that is and has been is but the twilight of the dawn. It is possible to believe all that the human mind has ever accomplished is but the dream before the awakening."

Thought is the causative force in life. It precedes physical manifestation. The idea exists before the invention, the plan or the results. Thomas Jefferson said, "If nature has made any one thing less susceptible than all others of exclusive property, it is the action of the thinking power called an idea."

While thought can be enormously powerful—allowing us humans to create something from nothing; to create a new world and transcend our beliefs, conditions and circumstances—it can also serve our addictions and dysfunctions and perpetuate our misery. One way the human mind does this is by converting all human experience into a simple idea it can comprehend. This can rob a profound experience of all its beauty and mystery, reducing it to a mere bit of two-dimensional copy.

The enemies of any large-scale transformation are many. Some are things we do and some are things we tolerate that preclude the possibility of transformation. Some are proactive and some are passive. Some are saying something and some are saying nothing. Merely ceasing to behave in some ways and starting to do different things won't have maximum impact if our consciousness—the frame within which we think—isn't transformed. Here is a brief list of some of these enemies:

Addictions of all kinds

Advocating and supporting market fundamentalism

Allowing our natural environment to deteriorate

Avoidance of matters of importance

Being inauthentic or condoning it in others

Blaming, scapegoating, litigiousness

Busy-ness, hurry

Chronic debt

Comfort-seeking, consolations, ego-payoffs

Complaining

Cynicism, abdication of personal responsibility

Denial

Disingenuousness

Exaggerated individualism, celebrity or specialness

Exaggerated persona, false images

Fatalism

Fundamentalism of all sorts

Gossip, particularly talk that diminishes anyone

Ignorance about systems thinking and how systems work or don't work

Immaturity, perpetual adolescence

Indulging our egos

Multitasking

Rankism of any kind (intolerance, racism, sexism, ageism, bossism, etc.)

Refusal to engage in inquiring dialogue

Relying exclusively on mass media for information

Repressed or suppressed emotions

Rudeness

Seeking or maintaining personal identity in anything external

Spiritual laziness
Taking any vengeance-based action, seeking revenge
Tolerating dysfunctional behavior, in people and organizations
Tolerating stress

The reality we experience in the world today is the result of our consciousness. This consciousness is expressed in many negative ways, as the partial list above illustrates. To shift our consciousness we must understand the dynamics of our pathologies. To understand our pathologies we must study them and become somewhat familiar with them so we can recognize them when they surface, which they are almost certainly going to do from time to time. I wish to spotlight in some depth two of the most egregious: fundamentalist thinking in all its modalities, and the obsessive thinking behind addictions of all kinds. While these explorations may trigger some discomfort, they will allow us to recognize these pathologies so we can avoid them in the future.

FUNDAMENTALISM: SYMPTOM OF THE GREAT DISCONNECT

The person who is most prone to becoming a fundamentalist is the person who is emotionally and intellectually attached to his or her beliefs about how things are supposed to be. Their worlds are black and white and are based on a "strict interpretation" (usually created by someone else) rather than on first-hand experience.

Fundamentalists adhere strictly to some dogma or doctrine in lieu of the context in which it is embodied. They can be intolerant of any views that do not agree with theirs, and sometimes demand that others believe exactly what they believe. There are conservative, liberal and middle-of-the-road fundamentalists. Their beliefs—whether it is the Bible, the Koran, or the Talmud in religion, or Smith's invisible hand, free-market capitalism, or Marx's manifesto for communism—attach to the content of the dogma instead of to any direct knowing or integration of personal experience.

Fundamentalists can be blindly loyal to their dogma—"the one and only truth"—refusing to question or challenge the status quo or the interpretation they have come to believe in. They are committed ideologues, and their fanaticism can usually be triggered quite easily. They resort readily to defensiveness and proselytizing whenever they feel challenged about their beliefs. These are the evangelists we hear about in a religious context, but there are also evangelical capitalists, doctors, academics, and lawyers who loudly proclaim their righteousness, regardless of the discipline in which they function.

Some fundamentalists keep their beliefs to themselves as a private matter. Others are more public about them. Taking our cue from Bob Fuller, these are the fundamentalist "rankists," who feel superior to anyone who doesn't share their beliefs.

In an ironic twist, fundamentalism is a form of idolatry, idolizing some "thing," usually in print: text, passages, words. Loyalty to the "thing" becomes fanatical in the extreme, like the Hitler Youth during World War II and suicide bombers of the present day.

Using German philosopher Martin Buber's terminology, fundamentalists have an "I—It" relationship with their religion, or ideology, or whatever else they might be idolizing, instead of an "I—Thou" embodiment of the underlying principles or context. The words or forms are taken quite literally by the fundamentalist.

Fundamentalism is linear, not holistic or systemic. It is competitive, not collaborative, and often excludes more than it includes. There is little room for metaphor or nuance in fundamentalism. Everything is interpreted literally, usually with a subjective spin or interpretation. Fundamentalism is a closed system. Deepak Chopra once referred to this as "psychosis of the soul."

Another characteristic of fundamentalism: there is an attempt to make the belief absolute, which of course it cannot be. But the fundamentalist still tries. Truth is absolute; it is one's direct experience. But beliefs can only be relative.

What fosters fundamentalism? Why has it become so rampant in the world in recent years and such a threat to humanity's survival? There are several feeders to which I can point. One is the culture of fear in which we are living, discussed in some detail in previous pages. Fear leads to choices that are consoling and easy to make. Anything that alleviates the fear is an "easy sell." The sense of certainty that fundamentalism offers can mask the fear of the unknown. Scarcity also fosters fundamentalism. The perception or belief that there isn't enough for everyone (love, money, food, land, etc.) feeds the fear that fosters the "easy out" that fundamentalism seems to promise. It is a sort of vacation from the continuing inquiry and scholarship required to maintain connection with the source experience, be that God, a Higher Power, nature, justice, medicine, politics, business or whatever. Other things that foster fundamentalism can include convenience, stress, and laziness. In the West, ease and convenience rule us. Fundamentalism is essentially another adolescent trait which provides what appears to be a shortcut to a convenient "truth," thus avoiding the rigor of study, exploration and apparent paradox. When people get caught up in fundamentalism of any type, their common beliefs tend to homogenize them, so they conform to a common ideal and, therefore, feel as if they are with "kindred spirits"—often in an "us versus them" sort of subculture. In a society that values "being right" as highly as the industrialized Western cultures do these days, this perceived benefit to our egos could be another payoff for fundamentalism of all sorts. However, satisfying one's need to belong or the need to be "right" in exchange for direct knowing is a huge sacrifice of one's uniqueness.

Religious Fundamentalism

One of the best descriptions I've read about the root of religious fundamentalism was stated by civil rights activist Reverend Howard

Thurman, who was interviewed in the late 1970s for a BBC feature on religion. Here's what he told the interviewer:

> I say that creeds, dogmas, and theologies are inventions of the mind. It is the nature of the mind to make sense out of experience, to reduce the conglomerates of experience to units of comprehension which we call principles, or ideologies, or concepts. Religious *experience* is dynamic, fluid, effervescent, yeasty. But the mind can't handle these so it has to imprison religious experience in some way, get it bottled up. Then, when the experience quiets down, the mind draws a bead on it and extracts concepts, notions, dogmas, so that religious experience can make sense to the mind. Meanwhile religious experience goes on *experiencing,* so that by the time I get my dogma stated so that I can think about it, the religious experience becomes an object of thought. When that happens, the experience goes on "experiencing."
>
> Therefore, whatever creed there is, whatever theology there is, must always be a little out of date. The genius of religious experience, it seems to me, is this: it has to have an altar. The mind demands that experience be reduced to manageable units so we can think about it. But, in order for the experience to remain vital, the altar has to be torn down and a new one built. The mind wants to be stabilized, it wants to get something settled once and for all. It is not the nature of religious experience to be stabilized. As long as the experience is vital, the only way it can spread is by contagion—not by instruction, not by addressing the mind, but something one person can catch from another, as you catch the measles.

> It's the nature of religious experience, it seems to me, of whatever kind, to be fluid, dynamic, moving, surging; it is the nature of the mind to hold things so that there can be a handle. An object of thought must have a this-ness and a that-ness dimension. This is the way the mind works, but life is not lived that way.[1]

Nineteenth-century Anglican Cardinal Newman said, "It is the very energy of thought which keeps thee from thy God." For me, religious fundamentalism is an attempt to comprehend that which cannot be comprehended, to rationalize the unfathomable, "effing" the ineffable. It is the human mind doing what it is supposed to do—making sense of things. But some things are ineffable and attempts to make sense of them are fruitless unless one is willing to settle for any explanation just to have one. Again, this goes for business, law, medicine, politics, even romance—anything, not just religion.

German theologian Willigis Jaeger describes fundamentalism as "nothing more than a desperate search for a true home by people who have lost their orientation in life. Fundamentalism promises believers salvation according to the motto: 'When you do this and this, and conform faithfully and piously to the rules of the community, you will go to heaven.' Many fundamentalist sects have had considerable success with this strategy, although the people who join them have been helped precious little."[2]

Science & Theology News reviewed the book *The Psychology of Religious Fundamentalism* and translates the authors' definition of fundamentalism as beliefs "based on a single sacred text that cannot be modified by other cultural or intellectual points of view." Single-sourceness and inflexibility appear to be the primary attributes of this mindset, according to the authors. Although published within the context of religion, the words do a pretty fair job of defining fundamentalism of all kinds.

Commentator-essayist Adam Gopnik wrote a book review of *The Gospel of Judas* in *The New Yorker* magazine in which he writes, "[I]t is useful to be reminded, in a time of renewed fundamentalism, that religions actually have no fundament: that the inerrant texts and unchallenged holies of any faith are the work of men and time."

William Sloan Coffin, former chaplain of Yale University, observed that religious fundamentalists "prefer certainty to truth." I participated in a public inquiry into fundamentalism in 2006 with Dean Alan Jones of Grace Cathedral in San Francisco, who shared, "We live in a fundamentalist culture . . . yet religion is supposed to deepen questions, not give answers."

Fundamentalism in Business

The One and Only Truth syndrome was fueled in the business world by selective repetition of Adam Smith's "free market" and "invisible hand" phraseologies, which for some meant unrestrained commerce. Of course, Smith could hardly have anticipated the scale of the market today: the securitization of everything, mass advertising (particularly the power of television), neuromarketing (the use of medical technologies to learn what makes consumers buy things so they can be better manipulated), financial persuasion of government officials (lobbying, campaign contributions and bribery), "corporate welfare" (tax breaks, subsidies and underwritings) and other developments that tilt the scales to favor providers of goods and services in the past couple of hundred years. The market is hardly unfettered and free today!

When corporate social responsibility was being called for in the 1960s, the hard core "invisible handers" used the proclamation of laissez-faire economist Milton Friedman to reinforce their ideology. Friedman served as economic advisor to U.S. President Richard Nixon and was awarded the Nobel Prize, so he brought much credibility to the cause. Friedman called social responsibility a "fundamentally subversive doctrine" in a free society, making him a hero to the fundamentalists who wanted total attention to the bottom line.

He authored words that fundamentalist free marketers have used as their dogma ever since he wrote them back in 1962: "There is one and only one social responsibility of business—to use its resources and engage in activities designed to increase its profits so long as it stays within the rules of the game, which is to say, engages in open and free competition without deception or fraud."[3]

Like religious zealots who are convinced they have found the one true way to God, the bottom liners flocked to Friedman's doctrine with such ferocity that a form of "brutal capitalism" was unleashed. "Darwinomics" is one term coined to describe such fundamentalist ideology in business.

"Market fundamentalism" is a term popularized by financial speculator, philanthropist, and political activist George Soros. He writes, "This idea was called laissez faire in the nineteenth century . . . I have found a better name for it: market fundamentalism." The term is commonly used by writers of economic topics to depict exaggerated beliefs in the market to solve society's problems, much like Friedman advocated. It has been applied sarcastically to the ideology of bottom liners.

Jeff Gates, author of *Democracy at Risk*, writes:

> We're just awakening to the many flaws in the naive notion that money need only be accountable to itself. Adam Smith, the father of free enterprise, would be appalled at the way we've allowed money to run amok, converting the pursuit of financial returns into a secular idolatry. He envisioned not financial markets but an engaged humanity as the animating force through which the pursuit of private gain becomes a public virtue. Although global capital markets certainly display an uncanny capacity to seek out profitable investments worldwide, that search has left in its wake grotesque social inequities, oppressive political systems, and environmental tragedies. That's why, I

suspect, Smith advocated a genuinely *self-designed* system … Only a *people-based* system was, he felt, capable of reflecting the complexity of motivation, aspiration and purpose that make humans so uniquely human. [4]

Gates then coins a term to describe the current fundamentalist approach to capitalism: "disillusionomics."

The meltdown of the deregulated capital markets that started in 2008 is a timely example of the tremendous harm that can be done with such well-entrenched beliefs when it comes to business and markets. When systems reach a level of dysfunctionality, they will fail. Market fundamentalism has lost much of its credibility with the meltdown. Even Alan Greenspan admitted he "got it wrong" by relying on his beliefs. Unfortunately for those who lost record levels of wealth, this fundamentalist ideology was very costly for many around the world. Yet there will be those who still staunchly defend their ideologies and continue adhering to their positions in spite of this global calamity.

Fundamentalism can show up in many other ways in business, any place where there is a strong belief in the One and Only Way. *Fast Company* magazine ran an article about fundamentalism in business written by Seth Godin, who says fundamentalists are characterized by two traits: "They live according to a large body of superstitions. Second, they believe that they are right and everyone else is wrong … Fundamentalists decide whether they like a new piece of information based on how it will affect their prior belief system, not based on whether it is actually true."

Fundamentalism and the Ego

Any conversation about consciousness must include some exploration of the negative aspects of the ego, both individual and collective. It can be challenging to write anything about this subject that doesn't get psychotechnical, perhaps off-putting to the lay person. As this book is meant for the lay person, not the mental health professional, I'll try to avoid too much psychobabble. However, we need to become more literate in matters involving consciousness if we wish to transcend our conditions and circumstances.

The negative ego has been defined as the unobserved mind and separated self, referring to the mind's propensity to seek identification with something outside of oneself. Modern mystic Eckhart Tolle does pretty well addressing ego in lay terminology. He writes:

> Ego is no more than this: identification with form, which primarily means thought forms. If evil has any reality—and it has a relative, not an absolute, reality—this is also its definition: complete identification with form—physical forms, thought forms, emotional forms. This results in a total unawareness of my connectedness with the whole, my intrinsic oneness with every "other" as well as with the Source. This forgetfulness is original sin, suffering, delusion. When this delusion of utter separateness underlies and governs whatever I think, say, and do, what kind of world do I create? To find the answer to this, observe how humans relate to each other, read a history book, or watch the news on television tonight.
>
> If the structures of the human mind remain unchanged, we will always end up re-creating fundamentally the same world, the same evils, the same dysfunction . . .[5]

Our egos like thinking that we have things under control. They seek familiarity, relative stability, certainty and having things figured out. Taking a fundamentalist position is an expedient that allows the ego to think everything is cool. The belief one holds is essentially a choice to make no further choices. Uncertainty appears to disappear. The downside of the fundamentalist position is that it becomes a barrier to further inquiry. Fundamentalism is a sham created by the ego to appear as though everything is under control, that there are no loose ends and that everything has been figured out "once and for all."

Ego is at the root in religious fundamentalism as well. Jaeger writes, "From a mystical standpoint sin is basically nothing more than refusing self-transcendence, the refusal to open oneself up in love. To put it in another way, the basic structure of sin is fixation on our ego."[6]

Seem like harsh words? That's what the ego-mind might say. But does your heart know the truth of it? Really?

A Course of Love refers to the "acceptable myth" or fairy tale the ego perpetuates, refusing to accept anything more powerful than the egoic mind until we have "proof." It states:

> This is the insanity of the nightmare you choose not to awaken from. It is as if you have said I will not open my eyes until someone proves to me that they will see when they are opened. You sit in darkness awaiting proof that only your own light will dispel.
>
> You do not stand separate and alone. At these words your heart rejoices and your mind rebels. Your mind rebels because it is the stronghold of the ego. Your thought system is what has made the world you see, the ego its constant companion in its construction.[7]

So the mind rebels while the heart rejoices. What a perfect description of the present-day human condition: the heart yearning for the connection to something existential and ineffable while the egoic mind rejects the very experience the heart is seeking. Talk about conflicted! Sin? Evil? Let us look a bit further.

Imperialist Fundamentalism: The Ego and the Evil of Being Right

History is filled with examples of the human ego on the rampage. Nothing can be more evil or harmful than the unchecked human ego running amuck, especially when it expresses itself in the collective.

Nobel Laureate Amartya Sen tells us that when we identify with some cause, belief, group of people, ideology or movement we become capable of different behavior. We could have several or even many identities, or just one. However, the latter could lead to some dark behaviors. He writes, "[I]dentity can also kill—and kill with abandon. A strong and exclusive sense of belonging to one group can in many cases carry with it the perception of distance and divergence from other groups." This can lead to dehumanizing "the other" and ruthless behavior such as genocide in one extreme to simple exploitation at a more benign extreme. While identity can "make an important contribution to the strength and the warmth of our relations with others" inside our group, it can also lead to evil acts. Sen continues: "Violence is fomented by the imposition of singular and belligerent identities on gullible people, championed by proficient artisans of terror."[8] A modern icon of such a "champion" is Osama bin Laden. Hitler is another from a past era. Buddha said, "It is a man's own mind, not his enemy or foe, that lures him to evil ways."

The Roman Catholic Church knew the "truth" when it ordered people to be burned alive if their opinion diverged even in the slightest from its doctrine. The Church's narrow interpretations of scripture were considered "right" because the sinners were "wrong." So they needed to be executed. Being "right" was more important than human life! And, as Tolle points out, "truth" can be simply a story you happen to believe in.

According to Tolle, dictator Pol Pot of Cambodia ordered one million people killed, including everybody who wore glasses! He writes, "The Marxist interpretation of history was the absolute truth, and according to his [Pol Pot's] version of it, those who wore glasses belonged to the educated class, the bourgeoisie, the exploiters of the peasants. They needed to be eliminated to make room for a new social order."[9]

Tolle further explains this nicely:

> [Y]ou won't find absolute truth if you look for it where it cannot be found: in doctrines, ideologies, sets of rules, or stories ... Thought can at best *point* to the truth, but it never *is* the truth. That's why Buddhists say "The finger pointing to the moon is not the moon." All religions are equally false and equally true, depending on how you use them. You can use them in the service of the ego or you can use them in the service of the Truth. If you believe only your religion is the Truth, you are using it in the service of the ego. Used in such a way, religion becomes ideology and creates an illusory sense of superiority as well as division and conflict between people. In the service of the Truth, religious teachings represent signposts or maps left behind by awakened humans to assist you in spiritual awakening, that is to say, in becoming free of identification with form.[10]

Bob Fuller addresses the issue of fundamentalism thus: "Fundamentalism of the imperious bent comes in a variety of flavors: moral righteousness, technological arrogance, intellectual condescension, and artistic snobbery, to name a few. It tends to be elitist, strident, domineering, supercilious, and overbearing." He cites two examples of this imperious kind of fundamentalism: "the mantle of infallibility assumed by NASA officials who overruled the engineers on Challenger; the 'commissars' on the Nuclear Regulatory Commission who arbitrarily substituted their own judgment for that of the hands-on-experts at Three Mile Island."[11]

It won't work to criticize the people who are advocates of fundamentalist views, as many do today. This gets us nowhere and only results in further alienation. Bob Fuller writes:

When adherents to any fundamentalist creed demonize dissenters as immoral or evil, they're treading a path that leads to dehumanization, oppression, and in the extreme, even to genocide. When nonbelievers put fundamentalists down as naïve and ignorant, they are taking the first step down the same treacherous path . . . Inhabiting a post-fundamentalist world will not be easy. It requires breaking our dependency on "intoxicating certitudes," as it were, and finding our footing without recourse to absolutes.[12]

Former Roman Catholic nun Karen Armstrong, author of *The Battle for God*, subsequently pursued advanced scholarly work at Oxford University. Her work in the Middle East led her to explore the commonalities of Islam, Judaism and Christianity, and she was honored by the Association of Muslim Social Scientists in 2003 as a bridge builder between these faiths. She has researched fundamentalism and found it is rooted in fear. She discovered that fundamentalists get more entrenched when they think they are being attacked. The operative word in the last sentence is "think." Exaggerated entrenchment comes when there is a perception or thought that one is being "attacked." This might explain why fundamentalists get so agitated when they feel the slightest challenge to their credo, or even suspect one. This could be the genesis of that breed of zealotry than can kill, the "sin" Jaeger writes about.

Tolle points to the folly of making changes outside without doing our "inner work." He writes,

The history of Communism, originally inspired by noble ideals, clearly illustrates what happens when people attempt to change external reality—create a new earth—without any prior change in their inner reality; their state of consciousness. They make plans

without taking into account the blueprint for dysfunction that every human being carries within: the
ego.[13]

Rabbi Harold S. Kushner shares this tale, which I include here
because it describes the inner conflict so many people feel in confronting ego:

> I recently ran across a story about a Native American
> tribal leader describing his own inner struggles. He
> said, "There are two dogs inside me. One of the dogs
> is mean and evil. The other dog is good. The mean
> dog fights the good dog all the time." Someone asked
> him which dog usually wins, and after a moment's
> reflection, he answered, "the one I feed the most."[14]

THE EGO AND THE SOUL:
AN INTERDEPENDENT RELATIONSHIP

Much of what has been written, by myself and others, can
lead people to think of their egos as a part of themselves to be
exorcised, to be rid of. Alan Seale, founder of The Center for
Transformational Presence in New York state, writes about ego
and the relationship between our souls and our egos in a very
compassionate way. He asserts that the ego has "the enormous
job of protecting you and making sure you are safe." When it
resists or attempts to control things, it may be that it has only a
limited perspective to "ensure first your survival and then your
success in the physical world." He points out that the physical
world is what the ego knows, including the rules and structures
of daily living, largely because egos designed them so they could
live in accord with other egos. Seale distinguishes the role of

the soul as having dominion over "the vast, unseen, nonphysical realms of Consciousness," which are largely unknown by the ego and therefore feared by it. Similarly, soul "is totally at home in the vastness of possibility." Then Seale makes a very powerful distinction: "Without ego as the physical component of being, soul cannot have a life in the physical realm. And without the expansiveness of soul, ego lacks inspired direction. So soul needs ego in order to have a physical world experience, and ego needs soul for its big-picture view."

He reminds us that many people place enormous expectations on the ego to take care of the soul, but since the soul has the greater awareness: "[I]n truth, it is up to soul to embrace ego . . . The more soul can nurture ego, support its learning and growth, and give it the reassurance it needs, the more ego can begin trusting soul and its big ideas and desires."[15]

RECOGNIZING OUR ADDICTIONS

While fundamentalism is a paramount mechanism induced by the egoic mind to distract us from the complete experience of being human, we cannot intelligently explore the subject of transformation or a societal consciousness shift without addressing another insidious enemy—addiction. Substance addiction, such as drugs and alcohol, is only the tip of the iceberg when it comes to the amount of obsessive behavior driving most of the global trends threatening the quality of life for much of the world. I define it thus: *Addiction is a habit one finds very difficult to break which is detrimental to anyone's well-being.* This covers pretty much everything most lay people normally associate with social addictions.

Paramount social addictions by this definition include consumerism, workaholism and oil dependence in the West—all facets of the "American Way" that have been so effectively exported to much of the industrialized world. These and other addictions come at the expense of the less developed countries, which is where most of the harm is done, completely out of sight from those dependent on their addictions. Since the U.S. and its lifestyle has been such an influence in spreading these addictions, let us take a closer look at this nation.

ADDICT NATION

According to a 2001 survey conducted by the U.S. Substance Abuse and Mental Health Services Administration, the U.S.A. is a "nation of addicts." Americans live very obsessive and compulsive lifestyles—but "addictive"? Let's look at some striking similarities between people we normally associate with addiction and many Americans.

Being an addict means that the addiction dominates your life, whatever form the addiction takes. It has first priority! Alan Leshner, Ph.D., of the National Institute on Drug Abuse, says that addicts admit this as they start getting "clean and sober." We Americans are obsessed by celebrity, technology, convenience, opinion, gossip, violence and sex. So you can say these obsessions dominate our lives. We are addicted to fat in our food, gasoline for our cars, porn for our fantasies, and alcohol or drugs to numb whatever bothers us. We are the major consumer of illegal drugs and the largest user of prescriptive antidepressants in the world! These and other addictions run our lives to a large degree, just as they do for the drug addict.

Health professionals in the field of addiction believe addictions are caused by a combination of biological, environmental and psychological influences. There may be a genetic predisposition to the addiction. If there is any addiction in the family environment, a person could take on traits that could contribute to future addictive behavior. Stresses or curiosity may lead to casual use, which, in turn, can exacerbate these predispositions and move into full-blown addiction. Americans have had three generations since World War II to get more and more used to the obsessive, consumptive and technology-driven lifestyles we live today. In other words, we have been subject to environmental influences by our parents, who were influenced by *their* parents. Addiction experts tell us that children of addicts are three times more likely to become addicts themselves. So generational influences cannot be discounted.

Once people become addicts, certain common personality traits emerge, like "difficulty delaying gratification, self-centeredness, lack of concentration and impatience," says Patricia Owen, Director of Research and Development at the Hazelden Foundation. Ask anyone from another country for a candid response and they are quite likely to tell you that these four traits are quite typical of Americans. We hate delaying gratification. We are perhaps the most egocentric nation on earth. We live for sound bites because we're too impatient to concentrate on any deeper exploration. That's four out of four traits Americans share with the addictive personality!

Addicts usually cease maturing emotionally once they start living addictive lifestyles. A big part of recovery is picking up where one has been arrested in one's emotional development. Many addicts started "using" as teenagers and after a number of years find themselves in adult bodies but with adolescent hearts and minds. Thus, recovery includes growing up emotionally. America is perhaps the most adolescent nation when it comes to the way it behaves as a culture. We've been this way for much of the time since the mid-1940s, when we seem to have ceased maturing.

ENOUGH ABOUT CONSCIOUSNESS

While the mind is a powerful resource for civilized humankind, it can get us into grave difficulties as well. This is especially true when we give it full dictatorial powers. When we think everything has to make sense and try to cram every life experience into the rational bucket of our minds, we begin playing God. When we get obsessed and attached to our ideas—the output our minds generate every day—we enact behaviors that are unhealthy for us and others. This same power can be used for good or bad, constructively or destructively.

Simply put, we humans have an option in how we think. We can choose reactive behaviors and pathological responses to circumstances in the world and allow them to fuel the fears and separation we harbor, or we can choose to respond transformatively and hold a vision for a better world for all without the cynicism and other baggage we've been carrying around. Continuing on the pathological reactionary path looks pretty hopeless, while the transformative response offers hope without fantasy, life in place of suffering, and fun without the fundamentalism.

Chapter 4
CHOOSING TRANSFORMATION

Former U.S. Ambassador to the United Nations Richard Holbrooke used a phrase I love when it comes to changing our thinking about how things have to be. In a 2004 interview in *Leaders* magazine, the experienced diplomat was asked about people in the world he most admired. He replied:

> The greatest person I ever met, bar none, is Nelson Mandela, and I have gotten to know him very well. No man is perfect, not even Mandela, but he took history by the throat, seized it, and changed its course through a combination of moral authority, vision, strategic sense, practical genius, and a remarkable capacity for forgiveness toward the thugs who ran South Africa under Apartheid.[1]

It is time for us all to "take history by the throat" and change from a mindset that tells us the best predictor of the future is the past—an attitude that dooms us to being slaves of our history—to a transformed mindset that creates a future based upon what we envision for ourselves, our families, our communities and our world.

Vaclav Havel, the artist who became president of the Czech Republic after the fall of the Soviet Union, has something to offer us on this topic as well. He writes, "Planetary democracy does not yet exist but our global civilization is already preparing a place for it. It is the very Earth we inhabit linked with Heaven above us. Only in this setting can the mutuality and the commonality of the human race be newly created with reverence and gratitude for that which transcends each of us and all of us together."[2] This sounds incredibly similar to the vision of the framers of the Declaration of Independence and subsequently the U.S. Constitution which laid the foundation for the American Dream.

IT'S ABOUT "LIVINGRY" NOT WEAPONRY

Twenty-five years ago Bucky Fuller stated that it was now highly feasible to take care of everybody on Earth at a "higher standard of living than any have ever known." Here we are decades later and we are still struggling with the same problems. He writes:

> It no longer has to be you or me. Selfishness is unnecessary and henceforth unrationalizable as mandated by survival. War is obsolete . . . It is a matter of converting the high technology from weaponry to livingry. The essence of livingry is human-life advantaging and environment controlling. With the highest aeronautical and engineering facilities of the world redirected from weaponry to livingry production, all humanity would have the option of becoming enduringly successful.
>
> All previous revolutions have been political—in them the have-not majority has attempted revengefully to pull down the economically advantaged

minority. If realized, this historically greatest design revolution will joyously elevate all humanity to unprecedented heights.[3]

Bucky's term "livingry" signifies a new sort of revolution, not one steeped in guns and violence but one in which we take responsibility for the future we are leaving for our children.

CHANGING THE CONTEXT

Let me say a few things about context, a subject that plays a key role in transformational change, the kind of change I'm referring to throughout this book. It might be useful to define it since it has come to be so widely misused by so many. Context is the mental framework from which we think.

Since the word "transformation" became popular in the 1970s, many people have come to think of it as synonymous with change. But transformation is far more than mere change. It references a shift from one context to another, from one worldview to another. For instance, redefining how reality is caused or what the culture is for a company is transformational. The shift that physicists went through when they realized that energy fields and quanta were more accurate descriptions of how things worked was a transformation in thinking.

The primary transformation we're addressing is a shift from having our collective thinking based upon the material domain, or content, to seeing context as generative of our reality. This requires us to transform our thinking about reality, cause and truth.

Shifting the framework from which we think allows all the content to shift as well. It's not unlike sea birds that get caught up in an oil spill in the ocean. We can rescue and clean all the gulls and pelicans we want, but if we release them before the spill is cleaned up they will most likely get covered in sludge again. In this example, the ocean represents the context and the birds the content. We can change the *content* as much as we'd like, but if the *context* remains unchanged there's little lasting improvement.

Context is not something widely discussed in the West. We are far more used to and comfortable talking and living in the domains of form. Since form is what we're familiar with and comfortable discussing, we tend to constantly change, improve or expand the *form* but rarely examine what the underlying *context* may be. Context includes all the underlying assumptions, conscious and unconscious, attitudes, perceptions and beliefs. So if we simply find an oil-soaked pelican and clean it up for release back into the wild without locating and cleaning up the oil spill in which it got contaminated, we could be wasting lots of work, expectations and time. And the pelican would likely die next time.

Form supports context but shouldn't be confused with it. For example, the context for democracy is individual liberty and empowerment. A democracy also requires laws and rules for everyone to get along with one another. Laws and rules are forms, like elections and the structure of the government. In a totalitarian state, there are still rules and laws but they support the context of totalitarianism. They are designed to empower the state, not the people. Both contexts need form to support their existence.

Some think that purpose is part of the context for things, and sometimes it can be. If the purpose of a system is to amass wealth, for instance, the structure of the organization and the rules for operating will be different than if the purpose is to serve the public welfare. Some forms can be the same, such as the use of a corporate charter. Again, as form supports the context or purpose, if it works, then it can be used. "Context provides the meaning to content," writes Mel Toomey, who heads the Center for Leadership Studies.

Context provides meaning for people in their work and in their personal lives. When the context of one's life is love and connection, one is much less inclined to seek consolations or distract oneself. Trust prevails. People make conscious choices based on the desire for something positive rather than to avoid something negative.

What if the grand context of all civilized humanity were to shift to one of caring and acceptance of everyone, recognizing we are all interconnected and interdependent? What if we could learn to rely on one another, like family, instead of building isolated islands of independence? What if we could see ourselves as one big global family, different in form but the same in spirit, "all for one and all for one"?

When this happens, I envision great changes in content. Sharing would replace hoarding. Trust would replace suspicion. Love would take the place of indifference. Dialogue and conflict resolution would replace war. Heartfelt ideas would rank equally with rationality. Free choice would replace desperation. Compassion would replace hatred. Natural knowing would replace fundamentalism. Sufficiency would replace extravagance. As Toynbee writes, "Compassion is the desire that moves the individual self to widen the scope of its self-concern to embrace the whole of the universal self."

The Great Dream is about shifting the context from separation to unity, not merely making changes in the content. It's about thinking differently, not just thinking about different things. Shifting the context may go against our current thinking, which we have come to value so much in our culture. Many people abide by the *concept* of unity; what is needed is for us to begin *living* from the context of unity.

A change on this level will require us to think in ways that may seem heretical or treasonous to the consensus mindset. It will be revolutionary, to be sure. And I do not mean simply radical or extreme. I mean revolutionary in every sense of the word—not as a metaphor or euphemism but as in creating a whole new frame from which we think. When revolution is taking place loyalties get challenged, friends can get angry, and colleagues can misunderstand. Even family members may think we're nuts. These are all part of any revolution. Accusations may come our way from people we care for who don't understand what we're talking about, what we are aiming for, what vision we hold. The revolution in context may not be pretty, or nice, or even peaceful, for systems rarely change graciously. And historically, large systems have rarely changed without some conflict and disagreement.

As I've noted before, people tend to seek out comfort and become somewhat attached to familiarity. This is behind much of our resistance to change. Interestingly, we know that when amebas are subject to constant stress they die; but we also know that when they are maintained at a constant tepid temperature they also die. The conclusion is that 100 percent comfort kills living things as does 100 percent stress. Therefore, people who seek to have things comfortable *all the time* would be committing suicide if they had their way. Similarly, organizations that seek stability would put themselves out of business were it not for something occasionally stimulating or shaking things up. Governments that seek 100 percent stability in their countries or regions could be doing the same thing. Systems require occasional discomforts to stay vital, make adjustments, and avoid death.

Life has a way of going through cycles—birthing, growing and maturing, dying or transforming. The sigmoid curve below

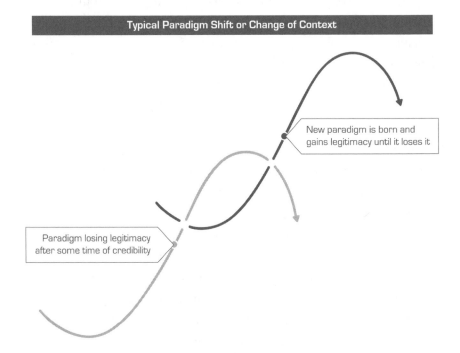

Typical Paradigm Shift or Change of Context

New paradigm is born and gains legitimacy until it loses it

Paradigm losing legitimacy after some time of credibility

demonstrates the life cycle that can apply to plants, people, organizations and even nations. The "rebirths" require that much of the old form and content give way to the new. Some cycles are longer than others, but all life is cyclical, following somewhat similar dynamics, as portrayed in the diagram.

When contexts shift, content adjusts. Once the context for anything shifts, content sorts itself out: existing content that still applies remains; outmoded content is eliminated; new content that's better suited to the new context is created. It isn't an "all or none" kind of thing at all.

Could a new Grand Context mean the end to all violence? Hardly. There will still be the aberration, the occasional whacko who goes berserk. There will be some who cannot make the transition to a new dream, a new context, even though it may be better for all involved. Shifting to the context of the worldview of all humanity won't deliver heaven on earth, at least not immediately. But it will allow greater functionality, sustainability, liberty and fulfillment to displace the dysfunction, violence, oppression and pathology. As the diagram below shows, we can create a reality in which a context of mistrust and separation with occasional incidents of love, connection and trust can be replaced with a context of love, connection and trust with occasional episodes of separation and mistrust.

Existing Context: Fear, separation and parts (stress) with isolated episodes of love, connection and wholeness (happiness)

Possible Context: Love, connection and wholeness (happiness) with episodes of fear, separation and conflict (stress)

AN EXTRAORDINARY CONFLUENCE

I recall the opening line from *A Tale of Two Cities*: "It was the best of times, it was the worst of times." Ours is certainly a time when that line is quite an accurate descriptor, for while we have plenty of reasons for alarm about our future, there is also a basis for optimism about a shift in our consciousness—a shift like the one Albert Einstein referenced half a century ago when he said we would never solve our problems by applying the same thinking that created them.

As a visionary Indian businessman once said to me, "It is wonderful to have a lofty vision that pulls you toward it but it helps if you are being chased by a tiger." Certain forces in the world, largely of our own doing, represent the tiger—pushing us closer and closer to a society divorced from its humanness, a future comprised of conditions that may have been unintended and unwanted but nevertheless are appearing in our reality.

Our vision for what we can be, and our continuing evolution toward a higher destiny, is what pulls us ever closer to the Great Dream. We are motivated to flee from negative forces while we are attracted to more positive ones, like a long train with locomotives at either end—one pushing us and another pulling. In the next three chapters we will look at some of the pulling and pushing forces that are exerting pressure on us all in these times so aptly described by Dickens a century and a half ago.

I've labeled these "Category I," "Category II," and "Category III" forces for transformation. While not meant to be a comprehensive list of *everything* that is contributing to this extraordinary confluence, I offer a brief description of *some* of the forces in each category.

Chapter 5
FORCES FOR TRANSFORMATION
Category 1: Forces Pushing for Change

The most unwanted or undesirable development that has occurred on this Earth in the past several decades—for most people—is that we have created the means to make ourselves extinct. It is sobering to realize that we could end up a few pages in God's personal journal about the failed human experiment. We can blow ourselves up several times over or we can irreversibly destroy the Earth's ability to support human life—perhaps any life. This makes for pretty dire dinner conversation, so it isn't usually discussed in polite circles.

Continuing on the paths we are treading today is both stupid and insane, completely against our self-interests unless we sincerely wish to die, ascend to heaven or be carried up in the coming rapture when the world ends. To continue thinking, "This is too big a problem for me to handle" or "Who am I to do anything about this?" or any other excuse for not making any course correction at the personal and societal levels is not only outmoded thought but is terribly irresponsible.

Shifting the paradigm of our consciousness is beyond being a really good idea. It is also imperative if we wish to survive!

What follows in this chapter are some brief descriptions of a few trends that are diminishing the quality of life for many of us around the world.

FATALISM

Growing fatalism about the future is dampening our spirits. Resignation and cynicism is growing in epidemic proportions. Acceptance of the reality we are in does not mean resignation about it. Acceptance of the way things are needs to come before any real changes can take place. Ending denial precedes recovery from any pathology.

In a February 2004 interview I was asked about the new "terror economy" in the United States. I told the interviewer that I didn't think it was anything really new, albeit more explicit. People were living in fear long before September 11, 2001, and will continue to do so as long as they hold themselves as separate from others and the world. But this disconnect doesn't need to continue if we summon a new kind of bravery. We currently have a major epidemic of this fatalism, a doctrine of mass resignation to happenchance. Fatalism is disempowering, which disallows hope and optimism for our collective future.

John Hopkins University physician Alex Scott writes:

> Fatalism may take the view that, if all our actions are caused by forces beyond our control, then we are not responsible for our actions. Fatalism is negative if it is a pervasive attitude . . . Fatalism can be a coping mechanism. Fatalism can be used to justify failure to oppose crime, injustice, violence, war, genocide, tyranny, oppression, and other moral or social problems. It can become a belief that nothing has meaning, nothing can be known, nothing that we do makes any difference. It can become a belief that nothing is worth

fighting for, that nothing is worth living for. It can become a rejection of any personal commitment . . .[1]

LACK OF RESPECT

Another trend people are unhappy about is a growing incivility or rudeness, particularly in industrialized nations. A trend in demonizing others has been growing exponentially in recent years, here in the U.S. and throughout the world, preventing or thwarting meaningful dialogue. There is a strong yearning among mature people to return to civility where manners are returned to the culture, not to such an extent as to be phony or overly polite, but simply to be mutually respectful of one another.

DECREASE IN LEARNING AND ENGAGED STUDY

We in the West have cut back on our scholarship or "adult learning" when it comes to new theories, ideas and discoveries about human behavior, the sciences, and all the other fascinating innovations and discoveries that take place after we finish our formal schooling. A few numbers:

33% of high school graduates never read another book for the rest of their lives.

58% of the U.S. adult population never reads another book after high school.

42% of college graduates never read another book.

80% of U.S. families did not buy or read a book last year.

70% of U.S. adults have not been in a bookstore in the last five years.

57% of new books are not read to completion.[2]

According to *The New York Times*, Americans spent an average of 1,580 hours watching television and only 105 hours reading books in 1996, and that latter number has been dropping in more recent years! In the five years between 2001 and 1996, the time Americans spent reading books dropped 12 percent.³ Could we be evolving into creatures who prefer to be "info-tained" (a hybrid of entertainment and information) or spoon-fed preselected and prepackaged information rather than study new ideas for ourselves? Are we opting for our media to deliver us our "mind food" like we've become accustomed to being served prepackaged dinners?

The U.S. National Endowment for the Arts (NEA) says that the number of adults who don't read any literature increased by more than 17 million between 1992 and 2002. Those reading any kind of book at all fell from 61 percent to 57 percent. NEA Chairman Dana Gioia stated, "We're seeing an enormous cultural shift from print media to electronic media, and the unintended consequences of that shift."

What about other nations and their desire to explore new ideas by reading books? According to the U.K.'s National Literary Trust, 40 percent of Britons never read books. According to research conducted by Book Marketing Ltd, people spend six hours a week reading compared with 23.5 hours a week watching television.⁴

With this trend away from reading books that require us to exercise our minds and think about new ideas, and toward infotainment which requires little discernment or critical thinking, we are running the risk of feeding our minds the same empty calories we have come to feed our bodies—substance with little nutritional value, bulk without nourishment. Could this be the McDonaldization of our thinking, feeding our minds junk food for fast intake? This infotainment may occupy the brain cells but is largely unfiltered and lacking in "nutritional value."

THE BLAME GAME

The growing litigiousness in America has led to a "social habit" of finding someone to blame for almost anything that happens to anyone who wants to complain. After all, lawyers have to make a living somehow. Lawyers also make most of the new laws, which is a prime example of a system reinforcing itself without any offsetting feedback. This trend also contributes to the atrophy of personal responsibility since someone else is always responsible, "not me." Very gradually, we've become conditioned to the "blame game," assuming there is always someone to pay for any pain or injustice we feel victimized by. This trend is eroding the sense of community we claim to yearn for. After all, some day we might be suing or being sued by the same neighbors who are hosting us at a barbeque in their back yard.

OBJECTIFYING OTHERS

Growing objectification of people is commonplace. It probably began long before Frederick Winslow Taylor entered the playing field as an industrial engineer in 1911 with the publication of his treatise *The Principles of Scientific Management*. Known as the "father of scientific management," his specialty was time and motion studies. Taylor's ideas dramatically improved productivity in factories and plants, but decades later he's been credited with destroying the soul of work, dehumanizing factories, and treating workers like automatons. I suppose you could say he dehumanized work.

It is natural for us to flow from *I-It* relationships to get things done to *I-Thou* relationships when we relate with other people, and to go back and forth. In our society, however, the I-It has become "massively swollen," as Buber calls it, so that domain dominates most of our relationships with one another. Perhaps this is due to the illusion of control we can have over this reality of usefulness and things.

Examples of how we objectify one another include thinking of people as "consumers" or "voters" or "shoppers" or "human resources" . . . well, you get the idea. Many men objectify women as sex objects, and in more recent years women have begun doing the same thing with men. We objectify our enemies so we can kill them in war without feeling any empathy or compassion. How many people refer to their lover as "my relationship"? Customers in chain stores know what it is like to be treated as objects; so do students in big schools. And what about people in the workplace? It has been suggested that the work we have created for ourselves is more befitting for machines than for people. New York consultant Sally Helgesen calls it "frankenwork," taking a cue from what Europeans call bioengineered food products: "frankenfood."

One of my favorites moments in film is when actor Kirk Douglas, playing Spartacus in the 1960 movie of the same name, screams to his Roman captors, "I am not an animal. I am a human being!" Perhaps workers in organizations should do something equivalent now, half a century later, and declare, "I am not a machine. I am a human being!"

TECHNOLOGICALLY MEDIATED RELATIONSHIPS WITH OTHERS

We in the West are getting more comfortable engaging with technology or machines than we are in dealing with other people directly. We are talking *at* each other in a manner similar to how we post a text message on the Internet. Some of us feel closer to characters on radio or television shows than we do to actual people in our lives. While we may see technological devices as a means to relate with others, our primary relationship is becoming one with the equipment, whether it's our cell phone, computer, PDA or iPod. Our primary sources of information come from machines like televisions, radios, cable and the Internet. Technology is the mediator of our relationship with other human beings! Systematically, we are getting used to relating directly with machines and only indirectly with other people.

LACK OF CONSCIENCE, ETHICS AND WISDOM

Western science has gotten so good at so many things thanks to our advances in technology that we've adopted a worldview of doing anything we have the capability of doing. The times call for discrimination, conscious discernment about what we put our energies into as a society, and awareness of whether our work, regardless of how well we perform it, is of benefit or detriment to the human race and life in general.

ISOLATION FROM THE COMMUNITY AND THE FAMILY UNIT

Today, I hear the constant complaint, "We feel so isolated and disconnected from our communities." Some make a sincere effort to reconnect locally, volunteering to work on committees or joining parent-teacher groups, but the natural community that existed before "suburbanitis" came on the scene may be gone forever.

In addition to the erosion of community as people began leaving the inner city for the suburbs, the family unit began to suffer. Dad wasn't home until late and wasn't very energetic when he arrived. Often, in an attempt to pay for the new costs of living in the suburbs, Mom started working. Over the next twenty or thirty years it became common to have both parents working "to make ends meet," which meant even less child-parent quality time. Now both parents came home late and tired, and the family unity eroded even further.

I hear it often and from many different corners of our society: the desire and yearning for being more connected with others, for a greater sense of community and "sense of place." Suburbanitis has allowed millions to own their own homes, but the price paid for the luxury has cost us more than just money.

The "third parent" phenomenon began about the same time, in the early 1960s, when both parents started working and television became the de facto babysitter. Kids from this era grew up knowing much more about life, the world, and events, making them dissidents in the mid-1960s who acted up at colleges and universities all around the world. The sexual revolution of the sixties, the Beat Era, folk music revivals, hippies and Haight Ashbury all added to the cultural earthquake.

ASSEMBLY-LINE EDUCATION

Related to all these other trends is the growing dysfunctionality of our formal education system. Our children are managing to beat the system and come out the other end without many of the basic skills and know-how we once took for granted. While this may be primarily an American phenomenon and mostly concerning our elementary and high schools, it will probably infect the rest of the world in time, as many other downward trends have in the past. The Industrial Age has had its way with not only our workplaces but also our "learning places." Peter Senge writes:

> [Our schools] may be the starkest example in modern society of an entire institution modeled after the assembly line. This has dramatically increased educational capability in our time, but it has also created many of the most intractable problems with which students, teachers, and parents struggle to this day. If we want to change schools, it is unlikely to happen until we understand more deeply the core assumptions on which the industrial-age school is based.[5]

OPINIONISM

In the West, we have become obsessed with our opinions—what I'll call "opinionism." One of the largest contributors to this obsession in the U.S. has been the evolution of talk radio into "shout radio." I suspect this is due to the repeal of the Federal Communication Commission's "fairness doctrine" in 1987, which provided an opportunity for radical programming that had not previously existed. According to Wikipedia, "Talk radio provided an immediacy and a high degree of emotionalism that seldom is reached on television or in magazines." Suddenly, what we thought about what was being reported in the news became important in the culture, particularly in the United States. Everyone is expected to have an opinion about many things. This is valued in our society. People today commonly spend time formulating opinions about relatively meaningless matters, such as verdicts in high-profile trials that have grabbed the attention of the public, or second-guessing what military strategies should be employed in the latest war. Our minds are busy generating opinions, like feeding candy to our intellects, while really important things that we could be doing with our energies go unaddressed.

Why do we do this? One possible explanation is that the separated mind does this to create an identity, to be special, so it judges and generates opinions about almost anything. Without judgment there would be no separation and, for the ego mind, no identity. It is as if we believed "I have an opinion, therefore I am."

Opinionism is killing us. Not merely figuratively, but literally. The more we live in our heads, the more numb we make ourselves. The more numb we make ourselves, the less likely we are to feel any concern about our future, collectively and individually.

IRRESPONSIBLE ATTITUDES ABOUT MONEY, DEBT AND CREDIT

The relentless commoditization of life in our society implicitly preaches that happiness resides in having stuff—that owning things and buying new things brings some degree of satisfaction and fulfillment. But more and more people are finding this promise to be bogus. After years of struggling to get stuff, we're realizing that self-fulfillment does not lie in commodities, be they cars, homes, jewelry, clothes, or any "thing" outside of ourself.

People's desire for more immediate gratification saw the advent of credit cards in the early 1950s. Our culture morphed from one that paid cash (for the most part) for purchases, or used the old "layaway" plans of the 1940s and 1950s, to one of buying on credit. Decades later, this new plastic culture allows for double-digit interest charges and record numbers of personal bankruptcy filings.

Another kind of plastic became a standard in American lives after WWII when this marvel of the age took hold. Plastic cups, eating utensils, poker chips, everything manufacturers could conceive making in this new marvel material, became disposable, and the U.S. shifted from a frugal economy of recyclers and reusers to being a throwaway society. Before the war, Americans recycled everything from scrap metal to manure to cloth. As of 2007, we throw away an average of 1,600 pounds of plastic a year per person, more than any other country in the world. While people may think recycling is making our lifestyles sustainable, only 5 percent of plastic bags, for example, is currently being recycled.

According to the U. S. Federal Deposit Insurance Corporation (also known as the "FDIC"):

> The U.S. personal bankruptcy rate has risen to a historically high level, from less than one per thousand population annually in the early 1970s to almost five per thousand population for the year ending September 30, 1997. This dramatic increase has been attributed largely to the use of credit cards to perpetuate consumer gratification. The FDIC bank trend report continues, "Aggressive marketing by credit card lenders or a lack of discipline on the part of consumers often are blamed for the increase in credit card debt outstanding. These explanations in essence argue that behavior has changed: that lenders have become more aggressive or borrowers less prudent."[6]

An August 2005 Associated Press report noted that U.S. bankruptcy filings numbered about 1.6 million a year, with quarterly highs exceeding 450,000 as the new law came closer to becoming effective. In October 2005, "the most sweeping rewrite of the U.S. bankruptcy codes in a quarter century" changed to make it "tougher to erase debt obligations." Credit card companies were a major influence in getting Congress to approve the rewrite—an ironic twist, given their complicity in mounting consumer debt.

Belgian currency expert Bernard Lietaer, author of *The Future of Money* and *Of Human Wealth*, believes the biggest issues facing humanity are "sustainability and the inequalities and breakdown in community, which create tensions that result in violence and wars." He adds, "We can address both these issues with the same tool, by consciously creating currency systems that will enhance community and sustainability."[7]

DIGITAL LIVING

Over the past three generations we have seen the birth of the atomic age, complete with the development of enough nuclear weaponry to destroy ourselves several times over. Technological development has also given computers to everyone who wants to buy one, a vastly different market from what IBM founder Tom Watson once opined, that in all the world there might be customers for five computers.

Bioengineering of food with all its blessings and curses, in addition to cloning and other controversial technical abilities we've developed , raise very new social questions, giving people pause for what is natural and right and what presents moral dilemmas or "playing God."

Nanotechnology—the engineering of functional systems at the molecular scale—is suspect in many circles. Public suspicion took a major leap when Cisco's chief scientist Bill Joy wrote about the possibility of robots duplicating themselves in his widely circulated editorial in *Wired* magazine in April 2000. Joy concluded his article by referencing the possibility of "engineered human beings" who "may be happy . . . but they will most certainly not be free. They will have been reduced to the status of domestic animals." Scary stuff!

Former Xerox chief scientist John Seeley Brown addressed the impact of digital culture on society in a conversation he had with a high school senior which was published in *Fast Company* magazine in the spring of 2006. Brown recognized that "the digital world must involve new social practices before its true social and civic power can be realized." He also acknowledged that "one of the challenges we all face today is maintaining a balance between the physical and the digital—but the more important balances are between 'the now' and tomorrow and 'the here' and elsewhere." Brown's call for balance can be seen as an argument for maintaining our humanness in light of the digital invasion.[8]

In 2005, *Discovery* magazine reported that "workers' IQ test scores drop temporarily by an average of 10 points when juggling phones, e-mails, and other electronic messages—more of an IQ drop than occurs after smoking marijuana or losing a night's sleep."[9]

RISE IN TERRORISM

Ever since the terrorists' attacks in the U.S. on September 11, 2001, there has been a formally declared War on Terrorism. The phenomenon of indiscreet violence, this global terrorism, the threat of violence to noncombatants is not particularly new. The IRA had been at it off and on, with a big upsurge targeting British civilians in the 1970s. Terrorism started becoming more widely noticed around the time of the hijacking of the Achilles Lauro cruise ship in the Mediterranean in 1985. Hijackings, suicide bombings, and other violent acts by terrorists who don't discriminate about their victims have since become all too familiar occurrences around the world.

MARKET MYTHS AND MANIPULATION

One of the myths that might be debunked is that the "free market" is really free. It has morphed into a manipulated market. Adam Smith's idea of free markets assumed the town's citizens would visit the square where merchants displayed their wares and, after perusing their choices, freely choose to buy what they wanted. No one tried to convince them they might need something they didn't need, bombarding them with commercials. The selection of goods was all within what most people in the community would need at some point—if not today, perhaps in the next week.

In these days of mass marketing we have become conditioned to insidious manipulation, including the use of sexuality to play to consumers' fears, insecurities and foibles. Smith never could have imagined the degree of repetition and subliminal messaging that modern day advertising utilizes. As Andrew Bard Schmookler points out in his book *The Illusion of Choice*, there is a challenge facing us all as both consumers and citizens in this day of mass marketing. He writes:

> What is needed is a radical change in the balance between the pieces and the whole. To become truly the masters of our destiny, we need to effect a fundamental realignment in the relationship between the capitalist economic system, in which private actors take separate actions to pursue their own purposes, and the democratic political system, in which the entire community makes collective decisions to promote the welfare of society as a whole.[10]

Numerous people have twisted Smith's theory of moral capitalism and given birth to what has been called "Social Darwinism"—which is truly about the survival of the fittest or most ruthless. This philosophy was proudly and publicly endorsed by Enron's Andy Fastow, the architect of what were called "aggressive" accounting procedures (otherwise known as "cooking the books"), which led to the 2001 scandal and collapse of the giant corporation.

Another trend that began with the rise of industrialists in the 1800s was the growing dominance of the corporation in society. The general public had been so conditioned to think of the n as the major power in the world that it was easy to overlool but steady rise of power in corporate "statehood." The cat was let out of the bag in 1995 when former McKinsey & Company partner Kenichi Ohmae wrote *The End of the Nation State: The Rise of Regional Economies*. Once touted by the *Financial Times* of London as "Japan's only management guru," Ohmae pointed to the real source of power in the world, the institution behind economies and currency valuation, trade, political influence and regulations: the corporation. Four years later, Ohmae authored another book that expanded our awareness, just in case we missed it the first time. It was titled *The Borderless World*. Again, he pointed to something that was obvious once examined: the borders around nation-states were meaningless to the borderless world of markets, the playing field of the corporation.

Both Ohmae titles are somewhat self-descriptive and explicitly express what most people hadn't fully accepted: nations were no longer in charge of the world; corporations were. Some corporations conspire with governments to maintain an illusion that this isn't so—an illusion which probably ameliorates some panic among the general public.

One potential milestone marking the emergence of the corporation as the most dominating human institution in the world took place in 1913. It has been observed that throughout history the tallest buildings have marked the most dominant institution. Learning institutions were the giant towers for a while, then places of worship had their turn. In 1913, New York City became the home of the Woolworth Building, dubbed the "Cathedral of Commerce" because it was the first building taller than all the religious cathedrals. That year could serve as a marker for the shift to the modern-day corporation as the most dominant institution in the world. Today, virtually all of the world's tallest buildings are signed with corporate logos and names.

Capital investment, once a noble activity carried out by people seeking a decent return on the capital they committed to a company or a project over a long-term period, has degenerated such that nearly all committing of funds nowadays can be more accurately compared to casino gambling. Short-term speculation has replaced long-term investment, as our society's "rushed economy" demands bigger returns in shorter and shorter cycles. Day trading, creating no value whatsoever for anyone other than the person doing the trading, has become so commonplace that TV infomercials now promise to make ordinary people into wealthy day traders in a weekend course.

THE GREAT MELTDOWN

The subprime mortgage crisis became critical during September 2008, characterized by severe insolvency threats to banks, brokerage houses and insurance companies and a lack of liquidity in global credit markets. The U.S. Treasury announced a plan to address the problems, triggered by simultaneous meltdowns at AIG, Fannie Mae, and Freddie Mac, as well as the giant Lehman Brothers.

On Monday, October 6, 2008, the Dow Jones Industrials dropped more than 700 points and fell below 10,000 for the first time in four years. The crash was the worst since the Great Depression in 1929 and quickly engulfed worldwide markets as other global exchanges grappled with the domino effects over the following months. Washington passed the Troubled Asset Relief Program soon thereafter, but the full ramifications of the aftereffects may not be known for generations.

ENVIRONMENTAL DEGRADATION

Environmental degradation continues at alarming rates as "the system" continues to motivate people to act in their short-term self-interest—their own survival or their family's—instead of acting as a responsible member of the global family. Whether you believe him or not, one of the world's leading scientists, the man who discovered a way to measure the hole in the ozone layer, is predicting monumental and inevitable climate change and a significant reduction in the human population. Scientist and inventor James Lovelock, developer of the Gaia Hypothesis, says, "You could quite seriously look at climate change as a response of the system intended to get rid of an irritating species: us humans."[11]

The basic context for the human relationship with our environment has been that we are separate from nature. "Conquering Nature" has been an explicit objective of Western culture, as if it is an enemy we need to dominate.

People "go out in nature" as if it is someplace separate from themselves. Think about it: when you see a herd of water buffalo grazing on an African plain, or discover a nest of eagles while hiking in the mountains, or are fishing in a stream, you think of yourself as "being in nature" and bask in the experience. Returning to your home in the suburbs or the city, you feel separated, "away from nature."

But are we not part of nature? Aren't we just as much "nature" as the eagle, the water buffalo and the trout? Is our home any less a part of nature than the nest, the grazing plain or the stream? This perspective, that we are part of nature and not separate from it, is not only more factual than the myth that we are separate but it is healthier. We will be far better suited to coexist as "members" with the eagle, the fish and the water buffalo, the forests, the stream and the flood plains if we hold ourselves as related to nature and all her elements.

MENTAL ANXIETY

Widespread anxiety throughout the industrialized nations, particularly in the United States, has reached such proportions that several authors have written books calling this "the age of anxiety." Medical treatment, prescription drugs, even television infomercials offer relief for the millions of people suffering from acute anxiety.

According to the February 7, 2006, edition of *The New York Times*, sleeping pill usage in the U.S. is up a whopping 60 percent since 2000. *The Times* stated that insomnia is a side effect of "an overworked, overwrought society." According to *Fast Company* magazine (March

2006), Harvard Medical School found the numbers of Americans between the ages of 18 and 54 treated for emotional disorders jumped 65 percent between the early 1990s and the early 2000s.

UNCONTROLLED POPULATION GROWTH

The pressures associated with extremely rapid global population growth add much strain and tension to the existing forces for change. The world's population has tripled in the past sixty years. It has almost doubled since 1970. Toward the end of this chapter we will consider more about the issue of population.

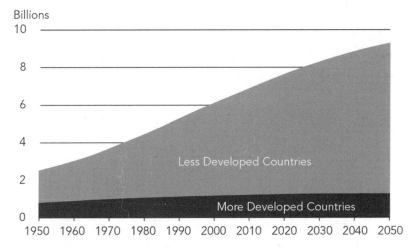

World Population Growth

Source: United Nations Population Division, *World Population Prospects: The 2010 Revision,* medium variant (2011).

ADULT IMMATURITY

The raging adolescence of the West is getting more and more conspicuous, particularly to citizens of developing countries. When asked about what stage of maturation we have reached at this time, audiences I have addressed all over the world agree that we humans are hardly into adulthood, but mostly still in adolescence.[12] Some even say that Americans are more adolescent than many older cultures, such as the European and Asian.

I'm reminded of the humorous observation that as teenagers grow up they become really surprised at how much smarter their parents are becoming. Similarly, despite our sophisticated technologies and financial abundance, more and more of us are starting to realize just how much wisdom resides in the teachings of the ancients—the indigenous people throughout the world who have preserved their ancestral values. This "ancient wisdom" has much to teach us about systems, holistic thinking, long-term sustainability, and appreciation for silence, solitude and ritual, especially rituals for passing into adulthood.

THE MATH AND SCIENCE GAP

According to *Popular Science* magazine, the National Science Board warned the U.S. Congress in February 2006 that the country is in a crisis when it comes to math and science. Five of their conclusions were:

- Sixty-eight percent of American fourth-graders were underperforming in math.
- American 15-year-olds ranked 21st out of 30 industrialized countries in math.
- American 15-year-olds ranked 19th out of 29 industrialized countries in science.
- Forty-two percent of middle school science teachers lacked certification in their field.
- The U.S. is granting half as many undergraduate degrees in math, science and engineering as Japan.

SEPARATION AND ALIENATION

Wherever I go, I hear complaints that people feel more isolated and less connected to one another, often accompanied by the lament that they could remember when that was not the case. Fewer of us have long-time friendships compared with generations past. Part of this is caused by the trend to have more and more transient relationships, those that come and go after a few years rather than those to which we commit for life. *American Sociologist Review* magazine reported that the percentage of Americans with no close friends increased a whopping 250 percent between 1985 and 2004. This is yet another indicator of the growing separation people are experiencing in their stress-filled, technology-occupied, consumptive lifestyles.

One way we separate ourselves from one another is through addictions of various types. One of these social addictions is watching television. In September 2006, CNN reported, "The average American home now has more television sets than people . . ."[13] That threshold was crossed within the past two years, according to Nielsen Media Research. There are 2.73 TV sets in the typical home and 2.55 people, the researchers said.

OVEREMPHASIS ON ECONOMICS

Economics has evolved into the most dominant system in Western cultures. The ultimate rationalizer in the everyday decisions we make is frequently the cost. Ballot measures in U.S. elections often include "financial impact" analyses so voters can consider the cost of their decisions to their city, county or state. People are influenced significantly more than in the past by economics. Many take jobs they don't like because the pay is better, and purchase certain foods because they are cheaper.

Speculation in real estate is another area in which investment has become displaced by the "flip mentality," whereby small entrepreneurs willing to take more risk purchase properties a bit below market value, add some improvements, and resell the property for a quick profit. This growing interest in short-term profit taking has permeated modern life in the West, from real estate to stock ownership to business start-ups which have their "exit strategies."

People seem to prefer making a profit by "doing deals" rather than by earning regular income. This "casino mentality" might best be summed up by pool hustler "Fast Eddie" (played by actor Paul Newman) in the movie *The Color of Money*, who quipped, "Money won is better than money earned." Even extremely rich people get excited winning a paltry twenty dollars on the golf course. This excitement seems to be a function of the thrill of winning—something like the high a gambler gets when playing for large stakes.

THE WEALTH GAP

One of the most insidious yet powerful forces pushing us toward the awful truth that our way of life is not sustainable for even the short term is the widening gap between the haves and have-nots. In 1960, the "wealth gap" was astonishing—the top 20 percent owned thirty times more than the bottom 20 percent of the population. However, in the past forty years even that enormous gap has almost tripled! This gap is increasing at an alarming rate and it is accelerating. It is entirely possible that our future could soon include one lone walled community containing all the rich and powerful people, with all their possessions, weaponry and militias, defending their fortress-like compound from the desperate billions who have nothing to live for and who are completely dedicated to the annihilation of the people and things within those walls.

A *USA Today* headline in December 2006 announced: "Rich still getting wealthier." According to the article:

> The richest two percent of adults still own more than half of the world's household wealth, perpetuating a yawning global gap between rich and poor. The World Institute for Development Economics Research in Finland reported that the richest one percent of adults owned 40 percent of global assets in 2000 . . . The richest 10 percent of adults accounted for 85 percent

of assets contrasted with the poorest 50 percent owning barely one percent of the world's wealth.[14]

One of the glaringly apparent indications of this widening gap
is the increasing ratio of CEO compensation to that of lower-
paid workers in the same company. A source of great angst in the
1980s, when people started becoming aware of huge discrepancies
in the U.S. compared to other industrialized economies like Japan,
the gap continues to grow nonetheless. *Forbes* magazine reports
that American CEO compensation increased 38 percent in 2006.
Congressional Research Service reports the pay ratio of CEOs to
the average worker has doubled since 1999, to a ratio of 179:1.

Vaclav Havel writes, "Our social and economic statistics are telling us what we already know in our hearts: we have created a world
that works for only a few. To change this, we must learn to act toward
each other and our environment in profoundly different ways."[15]

According to the *2004 World Wealth Report* compiled by Merrill
Lynch (the world's largest stockbroker) and the consulting firm
Capgemini, the assets of the wealthy elite grew to US$28.8 trillion

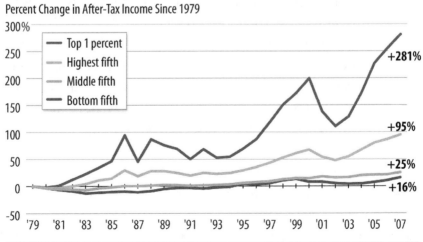

Income Gains at the Top Dwarf Those of Low- and Middle-Income Households
Percent Change in After-Tax Income Since 1979

Source: CBPP calculations from Congressional Budget Office data.   cbpp.org

in 2003, an increase of 7.7 percent over 2002. The measured wealth of the "ultra-rich" (those with over $30 million of liquid assets) was US$2.8 trillion of assets, indicating that nearly 10 percent of the total was in the hands of the rich. This ultra-rich category included some 70,000 people worldwide, less than one percent of the normal rich. According to the report, the accumulation of wealth by the rich and ultra-rich had no end in sight.

Jeff Gates cites some pretty shocking facts, developments over recent years that are certainly adding to the pressures to dramatically change our society. These are mostly statistics from the U.S. but I'm sure they have their counterparts in the rest of the industrialized world. Gates notes:

- The financial wealth of the top one percent of U.S. households now exceeds the combined wealth of the bottom 95 percent.
- From 1983-1997, only the top five percent of U.S. households saw an increase in their net worth while wealth declined for everyone else.
- For the first time since the Great Depression, the U.S. national savings rate turned negative (during the first quarter of 1999).
- On an inflation-adjusted basis, the median U.S. hourly wage in 1998 was 7 percent lower than in 1973.
- The pay gap between top U.S. executives and production workers grew from 42:1 in 1980 to 419:1 in 1998 (excluding the value of stock options). Executive pay at the nation's 365 largest companies rose an average 481 percent from 1990 to 1998 while corporate profits rose 108 percent.[16]

Gates also covers some statistics concerning how monetary wealth has been divided in recent years, which are quite similar to current trends. He points out that Disney CEO Michael Eisner received a pay package in 1998 totaling $575.6 million, 25,070 times the average Disney worker's pay. In the same year, Bill Gates (no relation to Jeff) "amassed more wealth than the combined net worth of the poorest 45 percent of American households." In addition, Gates reports, "a record 1.4 million Americans filed for bankruptcy," which amounts to "7,000 bankruptcies per hour, 8 hours/day, 5 days/ week." And these numbers preceded the 2008 depression!

As a percentage of personal income, household debt rose from 58 percent in 1973 to an estimated 85 percent in 1997, reports Gates—a 46 percent increase in only four years. Americans are over-spending themselves into bankruptcy steadily and systematically in greater and greater numbers, with no end in sight.

How about statistics relating to the entire world? Gates, in many works, points to shocking figures suggesting that we aren't doing too well in terms of being able to sustain ourselves.

- The world's 200 richest people more than doubled their net worth in the four years to 1999, to more than $1 trillion, for an average $5 billion each. Their combined wealth (the top 7 are Americans) equals the combined annual income of the world's poorest 2.5 billion people.
- The UN Development Program (UNDP) reports that 80 countries have per capita incomes lower than a decade ago. Sixty countries have been growing steadily poorer since 1980.
- Three billion people live on less than $2 per day while 1.3 billion of those get by on less than $1 per day.
- In 1960, the income gap between 1/5 of the world's people living in the richest countries and 1/5 in the poorest countries was 30 to 1. By 1990, the gap had widened to 60:1. By 1998, it had grown to 74:1.
- With global population expanding 80 million each year, World Bank President cautions that, unless we address this

"challenge of inclusion," 30 years hence we will have 5 billion people living on less than $2 per day.[17]

THE SUBJUGATION OF WOMEN

Gates also underlines what many are discovering, that the subjugation of women lies at the heart of almost all dysfunctional systems such as overpopulation, starvation, famine and war. He cites how women in developing countries produce 80 percent of the food yet receive only 10 percent of the agricultural assistance. Seventy percent of women are illiterate. Half the women of the world over the age of eighteen cannot read or write. Women are even refused education in many countries because educating girls is considered a waste of money. Gates also shows how women who are educated, even a little bit, reduce birth rates. He writes, "For every year that women attend school beyond the fourth grade, the birth rate declines 20 percent." And his final statistic, equally shocking, is that less than one percent of the world's assets are held in women's names.

CONSUMERISM

The West—largely influenced by the U.S.—has become an overconsumptive society, seemingly using the purchase of something new like a palliative for whatever is ailing us. I often hear people who have just heard some bad news say, "Let's go shopping!" It serves as a distraction for many, like alcohol and overwork, and there are 12 Step programs for people who are addicted to shopping. Swedish cancer researcher Karl Henrik Robert saw parallels between the way cancer grows in the human body and how humans consume, inspiring him to found a global organization called The Natural Step. The widespread consumerism we experience today was made possible by mass-production assembly lines that allowed lower prices, as popularized by Henry Ford in the days of his Model T. While Ford succeeded in his quest to produce an automobile that the average working family could afford, he also succeeded in fathering mass consumerism, at least in the United States. Will Rogers, popular comedian and colorful personality of that era, was heard to say about Ford, "It will take a hundred years to know if he helped us or hurt us. But he definitely didn't leave us where he found us."

THE AGE WAVE

The growing population of seniors in our society is a trend that many people seem to be ignoring. U.S. futurist Ken Dychtwald is an expert on the aging phenomenon and the challenges this "age wave" is creating.

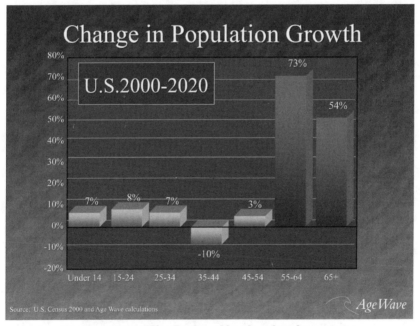

Graph courtesy of Ken Dychtwald and used with permission.

Compounding the rate of increase in older men and women today is the longevity factor. This growing segment of the population is also living longer. *Scientific American* magazine reports that 2005 was the midpoint of a decade that spanned three unique but very important transitions in our history as human beings. Before the turn of the century, writes author Joel Cohen, "young people always outnumbered old people. From 2000 forward, old people will out-number young people. Until approximately 2007, rural people will have always outnumbered urban people. From approximately 2007 forward, urban people will outnumber rural people." The article, en-titled "Human Population Grows Up," continues:

> The century with 2000 as its midpoint marks three ad-ditional unique, important transitions in human his-tory. First, no person who died before 1930 had lived through a doubling of the human population. Nor is any person born in 2050 or later likely to live through a doubling of the human population. In contrast, everyone 45 years old or older today has seen more than a doubling of human numbers from three bil-lion in 1960 to 6.5 billion in 2005. The peak popula-tion growth rate ever reached, about 2.1 percent a year, occurred between 1965 and 1970. Human population never grew with such speed before the 20th century and is never again likely to grow with such speed. Our descendants will look back on the late 1960s peak as the most significant demographic event in the history of the human population even though those of us who lived through it did not recognize it at the time.[18]

As Dychtwald, a psychologist, gerontologist and author of ten books on aging-related issues, points out: of all the people in the history of the world who have lived to be over 65 years of age, a phenomenal two out of three of them are alive today! In his talks about the longevity revolution he provides surprising statistics about the aging of our citizenry, information that doesn't seem to be in our present consciousness. "It is as if we are living in a 1970s con-sciousness about this," he said during a talk in late 2004, "deluding ourselves as to the consequences of this outmoded thinking."

In addition to the ballooning effect of the Age Wave, seniors in the U.S. have adopted an attitude of entitlement beyond their fair share. Already sitting on much of the nation's wealth, they continue to employ the country's most influential lobbyists for additional subsidies and benefits, adding to their disproportionate share. In an interview in the 2005 *Fortune* magazine special investors' issue, Dychtwald noted that the over-50 crowd has 70 percent of all the wealth in the country, and 80 percent of all the money in savings and loan institutions, which prompted the interviewer to ask: "How come they're getting all the discounts?"

CRISIS IN CONSCIOUSNESS

The forces *pushing* us toward crisis are substantial, to be sure. It is an historic time. But it is important to acknowledge there are also attracting forces *pulling* us toward this collective choicepoint. Social scientist Duane Elgin has this to say:

> We are moving into a time of steel-gripped necessity—a time of intense, planetary compression. In this generation, the world will become a superheated pressure cooker; the human family will be crushed by unrelenting forces that are so unyielding, and the stresses they place upon our world so extreme, that human civilization will soon either descend into chaos, or ascend in a spiraling process of profound transformation. On the one hand, if humanity is unwilling to work for the advance of all, then the world will collapse into a spiral of resource wars and misery, poverty, and calamity will descend on the planet.

Obviously Elgin paints a pretty ugly picture for the future. But he offers an optimistic outlook if we choose it. He continues:

On the other hand, unprecedented suffering may awaken humanity by burning through the unconscious denial, greed, and fear that now divide us. In encountering ourselves so directly and powerfully a new human alloy may emerge from the furnace of these superheated decades. Our time of fiery transition may fuse the human family together with a new sense of identity that is strong enough to support the building of a sustainable global cilization.[19]

The pushing and the pulling forces are helping us forge that "new human alloy." The next two chapters will highlight some of those forces of attraction.

TECHNOLOGICAL IMPACT

Before we engage the next category of forces, those external ones that are attracting us to them, let me point to one factor that deserves to be in *both* categories—those pushing us and those pulling us toward societal transformation. Technology can be our best friend or our worst enemy. After all, technology has no allegiances, no agenda, no moral compass. Technology merely enables its users to do whatever they want to do with greater ease and speed.

When Intel produced the first single-chip microprocessor in the early 1970s, a new level of technological revolution got underway, something akin to adding a jet engine to the propeller-driven airplane of the century-old Industrial Revolution. This new industry—that began with transistors and printed circuits—got labeled "high tech," and the world hasn't been the same since!

While we can solve our problems faster than ever before, provided we have a correct solution, we can also accelerate faster toward disaster. We can use technology to enable people all over the world to learn about things that would be useful for them, or we can use it to oppress more people, tell greater numbers of lies, or turn loose a lie with greater speed and scope than ever before. The same technology that has brought us the Internet and cellular communications has also allowed us to build weaponry that can kill more people without anyone getting their hands dirty, making objectifying the "enemy" even easier.

If we are prone to workaholism, technology enables us to do even more with less. The same technology that helps us grow a World Wide Web presence for our charities enables sleezeballs to promote kiddy porn more effectively. Whether the user is contributing to the transformation of our society or to its decline, technology enables it without discrimination.

Chapter 6
FORCES FOR TRANSFORMATION
Category II: External Attractors

There are many new developments and movements that make positive change more possible now than just a few years ago. Some of them may be known to you, some not. Many could be called developments of consciousness or wisdom. Some involve technologies. Others are trends, as growing numbers of people are mobilizing to bring about some aspect or other of this transformation I'm describing as the Great Dream.

These are some of the external attractors that could be pulling us into a new reality.

EAST AND WEST CULTURE BLUR

In the past fifty or sixty years, there has been a phenomenal blurring of cultures between the East and West. One of the most influential exports from the West has been our version of capitalism, which flies in the face of many traditions in the East, causing much debate and conflict within those societies. Similarly, one of the chief exports from the East has been the philosophies of Buddhism and Zen, which fly in the face of many traditions in the West, likewise causing much conflict and debate. Both cultures have faced significant challenges to their most cherished beliefs and worldviews. These challenges to core beliefs of both East and West most likely have a role in the trend toward fundamentalism as hardliners on both sides dig in their heels and become even more entrenched in their convictions.

AN INFORMED CITIZENRY

One of the most impactful developments of the past century on human beings has been the incredible rise in content and availability of information that can be accessed by the general public. This ranks as a true revolution in human communications. It was not very long ago when only a few elites had much of the information or knowledge in the world and the rest of us regarded them like parents, seeking their wisdom and guidance. After all, they knew and we didn't.

While Johannes Gutenberg invented the first printing press in Germany in the fifteenth century, the first lithographic offset printing press was created in England around 1875. After millennia of a small learned elite having an exclusive franchise on information and knowledge, high-speed presses allowed more and more of the "commoners" similar access to this wisdom.

Things changed even more significantly with the growing use of the telegraph in the mid-1800s and the subsequent installations of the telephone in the 1890s. These developments shortened the delays in communication by exponential factors, from weeks and months to mere minutes. While the amount of content was limited, the rate at which the information could be delivered to the desired party was comparatively at light speed. Offset printing became the most popular form of commercial printing in the 1950s and is used widely today for reproducing mass-market products such as newspapers and books, which were people's primary means for learning prior to the Internet. Also in the mid-twentieth century, television, faxes, wire services and other technologies offered the average citizen even more content, allowing millions of people to know so much more, much more quickly. Cable TV added even more content choices. But the Internet was the revolution within the revolution. Within seconds, anyone with a browser and an Internet hookup can access just about anything. More than a billion people now have as much information available to them as a relative handful did fifty years ago.

This revolution in communication technologies allows citizens of any country to be incredibly more informed. It allows workers to know as much as their bosses do. These delivery technologies make it possible for almost anything to be known by anyone who has access to them.

ACKNOWLEDGEMENT OF HUMAN RIGHTS

In 1948, the General Assembly of the United Nations adopted and proclaimed the Universal Declaration of Human Rights, formally acknowledging that everyone on Earth is entitled to having their basic needs met. This occurred five years after fifty countries met in San Francisco to form the United Nations, intended to "reaffirm faith in fundamental human rights, in the dignity and worth of the human person, in the equal rights of men and women and of nations large and small, and to establish conditions under which justice and respect for the obligations arising from treaties and other sources of international law can be maintained," among other aims.

The growing recognition among thinking individuals and communities that people of the world are interconnected and interdependent is an emergent force drawing us to a new way of thinking about how humans need to live together. In the 2004 report by the U.N. Secretary General's High-Level Panel on Threats, Challenges and Change, the synopsis reads, "no State can stand wholly alone." It further concludes that "we all share responsibility for each other's security" and urges members to "combine power with principle."

The report reminded us of the 1945 founding conference where U.S. President Harry Truman said, "[W]e all have to recognize—no matter how great our strength—that we must deny ourselves the license to do always as we please."

The report concluded: "Only dedicated leadership within and between States will generate effective collective security for the twenty-first century and forge a future that is both sustainable and secure."[1]

THE SPIRITUALITY MOVEMENT

Since the late 1980s, a nonreligious "spirit at work" movement has become conspicuous worldwide, largely taking hold in industrialized economies. Through book and CD/DVD sales, spiritual retreats, growing numbers of spiritual teachers who are not ordained by any conventional religious order, even associations that advocate spirituality becoming a greater value in the workplace—in all of these ways this movement has proliferated throughout the U.S. and in many other countries over the past few years.

"Spirituality in the workplace is an emerging trend that is becoming a Megatrend," says Patricia Aburdene, coauthor of the *Megatrends* books. She points to the following U.S. statistics:

- 78% of Americans today seek spiritual growth, which is up from 20% in 1994 (Gallup Poll cited in June 26, 2001 *Fortune* magazine cover article on "God and Business").
- 95% of Americans say they believe in God or a universal spirit (November 1, 1999 *Business Week* cover story "Religion in the workplace").
- 48% have talked about faith at work in the past 24 hours (from George Gallup's book *The Next American Spirituality*).
- 60% of executives respond positively to the term spirituality (June 26, 2001 *Fortune* magazine cover story on "God and Business.")[2]

"Personal spirituality," says Aburdene, "has accelerated to such a degree that it is spilling into institutions and businesses, transforming them. Capitalism is at a crossroads—facing a crisis of confidence from the revelations of unethical practices of many companies over the last couple of years."

In his book *Shadow Culture*, religious scholar Eugene Taylor writes, "The widespread flourishing of spirituality appears to have a number of defining characteristics, the primary one being that the motivating power behind it is not originating in mainstream institutionalized science, religion, or education. Rather, we are witnessing a popular phenomenon of epic proportions that is at once profoundly personal, experiential, and transcendent." He calls this phenomenon the "Third Great Awakening" in American religious life, an awakening he claims always springs from a "shadow culture."[3]

The arena with which I am most familiar is the business community. I know of regular conferences and membership associations—in Australia, Europe, Canada, Brazil, Argentina, Japan and many other countries besides the U.S.—where grassroots groups have formed networks in the past decade or two so that people who are seeking more meaning and a higher purpose for their endeavors at work can find support, fellowship and inspiration.

In 1986, the first meeting of the Caux (pronounced "ko") Roundtable was held in Switzerland, high above Lake Geneva. "Fritz" Philips, then head of The Philips Company, and Olivier Giscard d'Estaing, then vice chair of the INSEAD business school, were joined by various business leaders from Europe, the U.S. and Japan. Working with other concerned business leaders, the Roundtable ultimately authored what is today known as the Caux Round Table (CRT) Principles, which have influenced countless business leaders all over the world in adopting a more moral means of practicing commerce. The Seven CRT Principles are:

1. The responsibilities of businesses: beyond shareholders toward stake-holders.
2. The economic and social impact of business: toward innovation, justice, and world community.
3. Business behavior: beyond the letter of law toward a spirit of trust.
4. Respect for rules.
5. Support for multilateral trade.
6. Respect for the environment.
7. Avoidance of illicit operations.

Stephen Covey, whose modern classic *The 7 Habits of Highly Effective People* continues to lead the bestseller charts, even among business executives, refers to this movement as a "spiritual renaissance taking place in the business world today."

THE 12 STEP MOVEMENT

While we recognize the growth of addictions or compulsive behavior in the industrialized world, we have also seen the development of countermeasures to that modern aberration. In stark contrast to our complete reliance on Western medicine or science to cure our ills, the 1930s gave birth to Alcoholics Anonymous, which offers an alternative to willpower or a "magic bullet" approach to curing addictions of all kinds.[4] A.A. introduced a nonphysical, nonhierarchical, nonmedicated means to curing people's addictions. And it is very simple: telling the truth to yourself and surrendering to a "power greater than ourselves." Herein lies some incredible wisdom for humankind in its "soul quest," and it comes from a most unlikely source: a couple of drunks!

The core of the A.A. program is the 12 Steps, described by A.A. as "a group of principles, spiritual in their nature, which if practiced as a way of life, can expel the obsession to drink and enable the sufferer to become happily and usefully whole." Medical professionals are not involved in the grassroots 12 Step movement that has expanded to include hundreds of addictions—drugs, work, sex, shopping, cigarettes, food, bulimia, romance and many other destructive obsessions—besides alcohol.

The 12 Step phenomenon has allowed millions of people around the world to reengage a spiritual relationship without clergy, religious text or dogma and many of the religious trappings that turned so many people off to God earlier in their lives. One of the main lessons I observe from the 12 Step movement has been that people realize there is a limit for what humans can do merely through their intellects and wills. A "power greater" is necessary for us to transcend certain well-entrenched ideas or beliefs or habits.

THE GLOBAL BRAIN

Peter Russell's 1983 prediction of a "global brain" (the Internet, World Wide Web) seems to be flourishing, so why not his prediction of a new "inner evolution"?[5] The widespread connection of so many people through the Internet and the global transparency of information accelerates all evolution. This may be one of the biggest developments affecting possibility and shared knowledge, since virtually anyone can know almost everything, making it nearly impossible for there to be too much of a gap between the uniformed and the informed. Such widespread information, which can become wisdom in the minds of mature people, provides for "the people" to have a much bigger role in their own evolution—to be self-determining as a species at an unprecedented level.

In 1991, European hacker Linus Torvalds created a new software which came to be called Linux. In an unprecedented move, he made the software public property, giving it to the computer community. This is considered by many to be the beginning of the "open source" movement. Thousands of programmers, without any compensation, have contributed to making this operating system the primary challenger to Microsoft. People work on what interests them, not on any assigned project. No one owns Linux; there are no bosses, no hierarchies. Problems get fixed when someone in its informal network finds an agreed-upon solution. And it embodies the four traits James Surowiecki, financial columnist for *The New Yorker* magazine, points out in his book *The Wisdom of Crowds*: diversity, decentralization, independence, and aggregation.

The Linux phenomenon seems to fly in the face of conventional wisdom that insists that people are only motivated by financial gain and greed. Torvalds points to what he gets from this: personal satisfaction, belonging to his "network of trust," and having fun.

SYSTEMS THINKING

In the late 1930s, the field of systems thinking started sprouting as critical thinkers began seeing that while our society had created many complex systems, we were still trying to engage them dynamically as simple cause-effect relationships. Cause-effect thinking has its usefulness. It is handy for dealing with simple relationships, such as those in the physical reality. Cause-effect thinking can work for building cars on an assembly line but it does not translate or travel to more complex systems issues. Trying to use cause-effect thinking to deal with complex situations is like sending a toaster repairman into outer space to fix a satellite. Human systems are complex and require whole-system approaches.

As it became clearer to people that we were in need of a new way of engaging the very systems we had invented, a new field of study was developed. It was named General Systems Theory. Systems theorists from different disciplines caught on and elaborated upon the theory. Austrian biologist-philosopher Ludwig von Bertalanffy developed a kinetic theory of stationary open systems and was one of the founding fathers and vice-president of the Society for General Systems Theory. He was one of the first who applied the system methodology to psychology and the social sciences.

I first learned about systems dynamics from Peter Senge in the 1980s. Peter's mentor is Jay Forrester, who pioneered the field of system dynamics: analysis of the behavior of systems. In 1956, Forrester started the System Dynamics Group at the Sloan School of Management at M.I.T. Senge went on to write a best-selling book on systems dynamics and learning organizations entitled *The Fifth Discipline*, which became widely popular among corporate executives and business people in the early 1990s. While the model of learning organizations took hold, and even became "in vogue" for some time, the business world never seemed to completely grasp how systems work, why they misbehave, and how they can be improved when they start performing less than optimally or become significantly dysfunctional.

An understanding of systems dynamics may be the single best thing humans can learn for our interactions with each other to become healthier, wiser and easier. Most people still tend to think in terms of a "magic bullet" approach to problem solving, which is a completely outmoded means of sustaining improvement in the many complex systems created in recent decades.

Senge calls systems thinking "the fifth discipline" because he sees it as the cornerstone that allows for a shift of mind from "seeing parts to seeing wholes." As he puts it, understanding systems dynamics allows people to shift from being "helpless reactors" to "active participants" in shaping their reality.

When it comes to organizations, consultant David Kyle, Ph.D. has a point when he writes, "The complexity of our current organizational thinking at the beginning of the 21st Century needs to be transcendent in consciousness or societal systems will begin to rapidly collapse ... [W]e must both transform this level of complexity we've created and create new integrated approaches that take us beyond the old pattern and modes of thinking and acting."[6]

THE SPREAD OF DEMOCRACY

The week-long demonstration in Tiananmen Square in early 1989 was an indicator that the democracy movement was alive in China, even if mostly students participated. With digital pictures awash on the Internet thwarting state-controlled propaganda denying the huge event, word was out, quickly inspiring millions of others to start making demands. Over half the nations in the world are now democratic, tripling between 1972 and 2008. The fall of communism from popularity mirrors the rise of democracy, so that today only five countries consider themselves communist.

INCREASED ABILITY TO MEET PEOPLE'S BASIC NEEDS

We can now feed everyone in the world. It is only a matter of will and distribution. There is more than enough food. Sadly, some people are being paid not to grow food, and we have surplus foods rotting away. So, while some people starve in one part of the world, food rots in storage or people are "incentivized" not to grow food someplace else. Our economic system thwarts both the attempts to feed everyone and the collective will to change things.

We also have the ability to assure clean drinking water for everyone. Again, only the lack of collective will prevents us from achieving this. In other words, the world has the ability to provide for everyone's basic needs.

VALUE SHIFTS IN SOCIETY AND BUSINESS

The beginning of "cause marketing" in the early 1980s and the founding of groups like the Social Venture Network in 1987 and Business for Social Responsibility in 1992 are only three indicators of a value shift within the hearts of many people concerned about the environment and social responsibility in business. There were seeds planted in the 1960s for Corporate Social Responsibility (CSR), which has become a global movement still gaining momentum.

Social healing has been developing as a process for dealing with the scars left by generations of prejudice, persecution and, at the extreme, genocide. Many argue that transformation is not really possible unless this kind of widespread healing takes place; otherwise, the unattended wounds merely fester and resurface a generation or two later, like the scab that keeps reforming until the wound is opened and cleaned completely.

Can you imagine the Grand Canyon being dammed and flooded and made into the Earth's largest manmade reservoir, storing water for Los Angeles and its endless appetite for it? Well, it almost happened! Thanks to many dedicated environmentalists like David Brower, and newspaper ads by the Sierra Club, Federal plans to dam and flood this scenic treasure were aborted in 1968. But it was actually proposed and considered!

DEVELOPMENT OF ALTERNATIVE MONEY SYSTEMS

While there is no doubt that all human-designed systems need overhauling in this journey to a new enlightenment, one of the most critical is the economic system, which most people feel powerless over. While this task may seem quite daunting, many people in the world are currently at work creating alternative systems that are more sustainable, just and enlivening. Many of them are working outside the conventional government-issued currencies and creating alternative community currencies that allow local people to do business with one another based on agreement that the alternative currency will be honored. Bernard Lietaer estimated there were over 2,500 such currencies he knew about when we spoke in mid-2007. He started researching this subject in 1993, and considers his estimate conservative. A couple of decades ago community-issued complementary currencies were unheard of, as you can see in his graph.

In the mid-1900s, E. C. Riegel, champion for people's inherent money power over the political-bankers, wrote extensively about how the money system works. U.S. monetary researcher Thomas Greco and others have been inspired by Riegel, who some called "the money prophet," and are furthering ideas that promise the democratization of our economic systems worldwide.

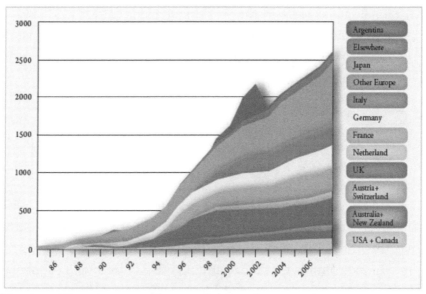

Number of Complementary Currency Systems Operational in 12 countries (1984-2007). Graph courtesy of Bernard Lietaer © Stephen Belgin, "New money for a New World" (Qiterra Press, 2011).

My point here is that, until quite recently, the general population assumed the only "legal tender" was currency issued by the government. This is changing fast, and consequently the banker-political-money system is losing legitimacy.

The late management guru Peter Drucker points to a very old saying: "Money knows no fatherland." Then he points out that the nation-state was invented in large part to disprove this. He explains how attempts to control money were at the very center of what came to be called "sovereignty." He writes, "But money has slipped the leash; it has gone transnational. It cannot be controlled any longer by national states, not even by their acting together."[7]

Lietaer, a former money-fund manager, sees not only the need for major corrections in our money system, but recognizes that a significant revolution is already underway, led by the financial markets. He writes:

A major shift in the world system has already occurred. Every government in the world, including
the most powerful ones, such as the U.S., is actually
being policed by the global foreign exchange market. If a government anywhere in the world dares
to challenge these financial institutions, capital
flight will almost instantaneously force it back into
orthodoxy.[8]

He cites *Business Week* magazine: "In this new market . . . billions can flow in and out of an economy in seconds. So powerful
has this force of money become that some observers now see the
'hot-money' (funds that move around quickly from one country to
another) becoming a sort of shadow world government—one that
is irretrievably eroding the concept of the sovereign powers of the
nation state."

So we can see that the nongovernmental forces are at work, en-
couraging signs that a free market will make corrections unless suppressed or restricted. Governments, central banks and those who
have assumed positions of power in the money system we all rely
upon have reason to be nervous.

In closing his book *The Future of Money*, Lietaer quotes from
the 1900 book *Philosophy of Money* by Georg Simmel, a brilliant
and prolific Berlin-born sociologist: "The debate about the future of
money is not about inflation or deflation, fixed or flexible exchange
rates, gold or paper standards; it is about the kind of society in which
money is to operate."[9]

With a truly free market comes choice. Therefore, we have a
choice as to what "kind of society" we want to be.

One of the most firmly established institutions worldwide is the
banking industry. Few industries are more entrenched in policy, procedure, regulation and tradition than banking. The cultural joke has
long been that banks only lend money to those who don't really need

it, thereby minimizing the perceived risk of loss for the people seeking loans because they have a *real* need rarely meet with warm receptions. Demonstrable income or assets that can serve as collateral are typical requirements to get the ear of a banker.

However, one man didn't let this stop him. Muhammad Yunus, a private individual in Bangladesh, started lending poor people small amounts of money—as little as a few cents at a time in U.S. currency. In 1976, he formed the Grameen Bank, which has become the pioneering model for an entirely new banking concept and market, now called "microcredit." Focusing on women as leverage points in ending poverty, Yunus spearheaded a movement to empower poor people who were being left out of the economic system simply because they couldn't gather a few dollars to become self-sufficient.

Both the microcredit movement and Grameen have grown enormously as a result. In 1997, twenty-nine hundred people from 137 countries gathered in Washington, DC, at the Microcredit Summit and launched a nine-year campaign to reach 100 million of the world's poorest families, especially the women of those families, with credit for self-employment and other financial and business services. Grameen now has 2.6 million borrowers, 95 percent of them women. The bank has over 1,000 branches in over 42,000 villages and employs over 11,000 people. Since it began, it has lent the equivalent of 3.9 billion dollars! Their recovery rate stands at 98 percent, and over 82 percent of its borrowers are also depositors. Impressive statistics any mainstream bank might envy.

Yunus was personally honored when he received *The Economist* magazine's Social and Economic Innovation Award in 2004 for his pioneering work and leadership. In 2006 he was honored with the Nobel Peace Prize.

In late 2008, the largest credit crisis and market crash since the Great Depression took place, triggering a global meltdown of staggering proportions. While the full fallout from this crisis may not be fully realized as this book goes to press, it would appear that the capitalistic system as it has evolved since the days of Adam Smith has experienced a major hiccup which could lead to a reformation into a system based less on credit and consumption.

All the factors briefly considered in this chapter are among the *external* attractors, reasons for optimism that will allow us to make an historic shift in consciousness and create the kind of world we want, to step into our next stage of evolution. In the next chapter we'll look at some of the *internal* attractors that could pull us into this historic shift to a sustainable, adult society.

Chapter 7
FORCES FOR TRANSFORMATION
Category III: Internal Attractors / Inspirations

This category is the most challenging to describe, since these forces are very subjective and much less obvious. They are internal motivations—internal for each of us as people, as citizens, and as members of this species called *homo sapiens*. Although such factors are generally the domain of social scientists, social psychologists, anthropologists and members of other scholarly disciplines that study human evolution, I offer them here, nonetheless, as they are integral to our treatment of what I've termed "The Great Growing Up."

These mostly hidden forces are behind why one person becomes a school teacher and another a musician, a tool and die maker, an architect, a writer, or an auto mechanic. These inconspicuous forces are behind why one architect loves to fly-fish and why some musicians love meeting new people while others hate fishing and are terribly shy in crowds.

Phrases like "follow your bliss," made popular by mythologist Joseph Campbell, or "fulfilling one's destiny," or references to sensing one's "calling" as used by the entrepreneur are attempts to describe these highly subjective experiences.

Throughout our lives we continue developing our values, even after we are deemed "adult." Some applicable research points to the fact that many of us come up with similar values independently, without explicit leadership. In other words, large numbers of us do change our minds about social outcomes. One relevant example is reflected in the work of sociologist and researcher Paul Ray, who in 1994 discovered a whole new subculture in the United States, one that hadn't previously been recognized. The phenomenon Ray identified was that individuals were changing their minds about many things in our society, starting back in the 1960s. He called these folks the "Cultural Creatives" and characterized them as being neither Modernists nor Traditionalists but rather integrators.[1] One of the chief characteristics of this integrative subculture was that these people were used to reframing or changing their minds. Most of them had been part of some social change movement like civil rights, women's rights, the environmental movement and/or the human potential movement. Their mind-changing muscles had been active, so they were not firmly wedded to any position or belief for life.

The big surprise in Ray's research was that there were already about 50 million people who fit this category in the U.S. alone! That was 24 percent of the adult population at the time, with Modernists and Traditionalists making up most of the remaining population. Furthermore, this new group was representative of the demographics of the whole country—economically, politically, and in every other way, except for two. Women outnumbered men by about two to one, and the West and East coasts had slightly higher proportions (5 percent) of these Cultural Creatives. This group is the only one of these three main U.S. subcultures that is actually growing, so that number would be considerably higher today.

Since there is no leader for this trend, Cultural Creatives don't know that other like-minded people exist out there. It is truly grassroots in that tens of millions of people came to similai con-clusions that "there must be a better way," *completely on their own!* This is where the collective will to create a different future than the one we appear headed for will come from—the general population, the people.

Once we take a look back at the past few decades and see how much we have learned and grown, along with what abilities and re-sources we now possess, it is easier to see the opportunity standing in front of us. But taking advantage of this opportunity requires us to take responsibility for our future. This may require many people to reframe, as the Cultural Creatives have learned to do, and shift to a different paradigm of thought about the world and the future.

Let's now look at some of the forces that may assist that reframing.

TRANSFORMATIVE LEARNING

A new way of adult learning has also emerged in recent years, what some call "transformative learning." Bob Kegan is a professor of education at Harvard Business School and a life-span developmental psychologist. He defines transformative learning as what happens when someone changes "not just the way he behaves, not just the way he feels, but the way he knows—not just what he knows but the way he knows." Canadian educator Patricia Cranton identifies three categories for adult learning: subject focused, consumer focused, and "emancipatory," which transforms the learner through critical reflection. In an article she coauthored with Laurence Robert Cohen, "Spirals of Learning," they state that emancipatory learning is "the personal, subjective knowledge of one's self, acquired through critical self-reflection."[2] This leads to personal empowerment, they point out, and the individual who critically questions his or her values engages in a uniquely subjective activity.

THE PHYSICAL SCIENCES AND CHANGING VIEWS OF REALITY

The West's sacred cow—the much-revered physical sciences—is becoming less sacred as we're learning that reality isn't what we thought it was when most of us went to school. Quantum physics tells us that what we were taught in high school physics was not entirely correct. Bell's Theorem (that certain quantum effects travel faster than light) led to wider acceptance of quantum phenomena in 1964, but there was (and in some cases still is) a lag in having it become part of school curricula. So our explanation for how the world works is outdated, which indeed means that "reality" isn't what we thought it was or what it used to be!

"Physicists have had to accept that reality at the quantum level can no longer be understood in a conventional sense," reports the Institute of Noetic Sciences (IONS). "The larger problem is that certain aspects of quantum mechanics contradict Einstein's theory of relativity, yet they both appear to be true. Modern physics is still trying to come to terms with this."[3] IONS reports that such areas of inquiry as string theory, the particle/wave paradox, and multiple dimensions in the universe are "higher dimensions" in science, and "are believed to be a means by which the fundamental interconnectedness of the universe—a primary feature of the emerging worldview—can occur."

One way new theories of reality can accommodate such fundamental contradictions is to question our classical system of logic. Says IONS, "Something is either true or not true. But this doesn't provide a complete description of reality. For example, according to quantum mechanics, a photon can act like both—particle and a wave."

For centuries philosophers and mystics have been addressing the abstractions of reality, long before modern-day science got into the act. The general public seems oddly content leaving this territory— the definition of reality—to the sages rather than taking the time or investing the rigor to immerse themselves in the paradoxes and seeming contradictions posed by these thinkers through the ages. Peter Kingsley writes about how we have failed to understand Parmenides:

> Ours has become a culture of convenience; but learning about ourselves is rather inconvenient because it turns the world we live in upside down … And with someone like Parmenides there are no shortcuts. We simply have to start at the beginning.[4]

GROWTH IN COLLECTIVE WISDOM

Greater and greater numbers of people are coming to the recognition that human beings are here for something more than simply working really hard and buying everything they can afford. More and more people are seeing beyond this present day production-consumption merry-go-round that "free market capitalism" has promulgated throughout the world.

Is it possible that democracy could be representative of a "self-realized society"? In *The Wisdom of Crowds*, James Surowiecki writes that "democracy is actually an excellent vehicle for making intelligent decisions and uncovering the truth." He then cites some of the research on the wisdom of markets in general, which include people who vary considerably in their understanding and sophistication regarding the issues. Citing economist Vernon Smith's work in 1956, Surowiecki explains:

> [W]hat's really important about the work of Smith and his peers is that it demonstrates that people who can be, as he calls them, naive, unsophisticated agents, can coordinate themselves to achieve complex, mutually beneficial ends even if they're not really sure, at the start, what those ends are or what it will take to accomplish them. As individuals, they don't know

where they're going. But as part of a market, they're suddenly able to get there, and fast.[5]

Along with all the other examples Surowiecki provides about the wisdom of diverse groups, he suggests strong evidence that the best democracies are those where the people call the shots without relying on experts to do their thinking for them.

Of course, giant nations like China, which remains communist and boasts of having over 20 percent of the world's population, and federal monarchy India with over 15 percent, dramatically skew the numbers when it comes to populations living in democratic countries. Nonetheless, greater numbers of people possess some degree of personal freedom under democratic governments today than ever before.

In *Leading Through Conflict*, conflict-resolution expert Mark Gerzon writes about a process Nelson Mandela went through to become committed to freedom on all levels:

> From this perspective, it is clear why some leaders can lead beyond borders, and some cannot. In *Long Walk to Freedom*, Nelson Mandela writes that he evolved from caring only about his freedom ("egocentric"), to caring about the freedom of his own people ("sociocentric") to becoming committed to the freedom of all people ("worldcentric"). This inner evolution of consciousness was pivotal to the historic and heroic role he played in southern Africa, and the world.[6]

THE RISE OF INTERDEPENDENCE

The formation of the European Union is another sign of new thinking in our world today. The Europeans, with far more history and arguably greater maturity than relative "upstart" Americans, chose to come together in a federation of their own design. First proposed in 1950, the E.U. was formed in 1973 when the first group of six nations formed the core federation. The E.U. is growing each year, with over twenty-five countries belonging as I write this. The underlying purpose of the E.U. is that each nation feels it will be better off together rather than remaining separate. As the Europa. eu website declares: "In the increasingly interdependent world of the 21st Century, it will be even more necessary for every European citizen to cooperate with people from other countries in a spirit of curiosity, tolerance and solidarity."[7]

First coined in the mid-1940s, the term "interdependence" started becoming widely recognized in the 1990s as the state of being reliant upon one another, as opposed to being either completely dependent on a monarch or other power figure or entirely independent. People in certain cultures, like early America with its larger-than-life Western cowboy imagery, craved complete independence and rugged individualism. Perhaps this craving was a backlash after centuries of tyranny and domination of royalties. Dependence on some forces was reluctantly endured when the individual recognized that certain things were beyond "one man's abilities." Even the cowboys of the Old West came to depend upon the market for beef, on U.S. Marshals for upholding law and order, and on the mail for delivering communications.

THE WOMEN'S MOVEMENT

The increasing influence of the feminine is a major factor in bringing about positive change. Following centuries of patriarchy, the U.S. suffrage movement in the late 1800s and early 1900s resulted in the passage of the 19th Amendment to the U.S. Constitution in 1920. It's hard for those of us living now to fully grasp that half of the U.S. population was not allowed to vote prior to this time, and women weren't given the right to vote until many years later in other countries. Women still can't vote in some democracies in the world! Nonetheless, this emergence of values and principles largely embodied by women is still happening, adding to the powerful forces contributing to the social transformation occurring now, whereas it might not have been possible or as easy a few decades ago.

While the industrialized nations have experienced lots of changes because of this rise in feminine power, particularly in workplaces, the developing countries are under pressure to treat women with greater equality and respect. While we have a long way to go before there is anything close to parity between the sexes, great changes have occurred in the consciousness of both men and women, along with big strides in legislation and culture, with lots more to come.

Besides gender parity, the women's movement has championed the value of the feminine aspect of both men and women. Gerzon writes about the influence of the feminine, citing renowned futurist John Naisbitt:

> In the West, because of the shift away from male-only leadership and the inclusion of women in virtually every institutional setting, a natural influx of new styles and values of leadership are penetrating our culture. On one level, these styles and values could be called more "feminine." In fact, because they embody the gifts of both genders, it is more accurate to call these styles and values more "integral" because they reflect the best of both genders. "The average male reader," observes futurist trend analyst John Naisbitt, "might greet the emergence of . . . women with a skeptical response: a trend, perhaps, but a megatrend? Surely not."[8]

But Naisbitt's research, not only in the U.S. but also in Asia and elsewhere, has convinced him that "such a reaction rates somewhere between ignorance and pure folly." He now claims that the "Emergence of Women" is one of the major forces at work in business and politics in the world today.

In 1995, the Fourth World Conference on Women was held in Beijing, capital of the People's Republic of China. Women from almost 200 nations attended. Concurrently, there was an NGO (Non-Governmental Organization) meeting on the subject of the advancement of women and the achievement of equality between women and men, not as a "women's issue" but as a matter of human rights and a condition for social justice. Together and separately the two conferences were the largest ever sponsored by the United Nations. The Conference forced the world's governments to write extensive reports on the status of women, raised consciousness in international agencies about the importance of a "gender perspective," and gave feminists all over the world ammunition for the battles they had yet to fight at home.

Rejecting the idea that matriarchy is the alternative to patriarchy, cultural historian Riane Eisler shows that deeply rooted in our earliest cultural history is what she calls a "partnership model": a more peaceful and equitable way of structuring relations in which—beginning with the fundamental difference between female and male in our species—diversity is truly valued. She then documents a shift from what she calls the "domination model": warlike, inequitable, rigidly male-dominated cultures. Most important, she shows that much of modern history has consisted of one challenge after another to traditions of domination—from the "divine right" of kings to rule their "subjects" to the "divine right" of men to rule the women and children in the "castles" of their homes. She writes in her most popular book, *The Chalice and the Blade*:

> Human evolution is now at a crossroads. Stripped to its essentials, the central human task is how to organize society to promote the survival of our species and the development of our unique potentials. A partnership society offers us a viable alternative.[9]

CONSCIOUS LEADERSHIP

In the past, we have seemed content to leave the future to others, to our "designated leaders." But most of our leaders are too invested in their positions to take such radical responsibility.

Since the 1990s I've been writing articles on what I'm calling "conscious leadership"—a term I use to describe consciousness in action, taking responsibility for what needs to happen in the moment. In brief, the conscious leader doesn't wait for someone to come along who's been authorized to lead, or someone who has been given a title that designates him or her as a leader. The conscious leader steps up when there is a need for someone to take full responsibility.

I mention this here because we are at a place in our evolution when many of us have the capability to know as much as our leaders and see things that others cannot. Therefore, we all have a perspective that can be quite unique and thereby essential for wisdom amongst the community. This requires each of us to be willing to take responsibility, to speak out, and stand tall for things we see that need fixing or things that call to be done.

Since consciousness includes mature wisdom with a holistic perspective, anarchy is less likely with everyone taking their role when they see something that requires intervention or responsible action of some kind, and only then becoming a follower if the situation calls for it. Back and forth, leader to follower and vice versa, with the interest of the whole always in mind.

In 2005 and 2006, two seasoned U.S. business consultants, Gary Heil and David Kyle, interviewed about 400 group leaders and managers and discovered something quite intriguing. All of the interviewees were quick to cite the principles of leadership they admired, even listing many of the same people in history who personified these traits. But when asked if they practiced these principles, they all admitted they did not. Instead, they conformed to the style of leadership their organizations seemingly demanded. In other words, while leaders *know how* to lead well, most opt for complying with the system to which they are loyal, in many cases doing the exact opposite of what they think is the "right thing." How's that for dysfunctionality in action?

THE HUMAN POTENTIAL MOVEMENT

Running parallel to the exploration of outer space which began in the 1960s, there has been a global exploration of "inner space," or the transcendent. The idea of people being responsible for their lives and their circumstances became a commonplace approach to personal development in the 1950s, fueled by the advent and growth of humanistic psychology, founded by Abraham Maslow. One of Maslow's most famous contributions is his "hierarchy of needs," which became popular with human resource departments worldwide as mainstream acceptance of the hierarchy grew, along with the idea that once people had their basic needs met they would eventually seek "self-actualization."

Humanistic psychology opened the door to psychotherapy as a means not only to improved mental health but to an improved consciousness. Prior to this time, people going to see a "shrink" were considered "sick" or as having mental problems or being defective in some way. Gradually, going to see a psychotherapist started gaining acceptance as a means to personal development, and this new legitimacy catalyzed the human potential movement a few years later. Today, very few people view regular visits to a psychotherapist or counselor as anything weirder than having a personal trainer for improved physical well-being.

Goal setting, meditation, uncovering core belief systems, healing past hurts, positive imaging and affirmations, eliminating compulsions, behavior modification, emotional maturing, Rolfing, massage, yoga, ritual and many other psychological, emotional and physical practices have become somewhat commonplace among individuals.

GROUP POTENTIAL

Standing on the shoulders of the human potential movement, organization development began becoming popular. Now known widely among business consultants and strategic planners as O.D., this professional discipline took hold in the 1970s. Today it is a huge field of practice that is quite commonplace in corporations throughout the world. O.D. involves integrating the individual with the organizational, applying many of the practices from the human potential movement to improve organizational potential.

Team building, participative management, leadership trainings, executive mentoring and coaching, visioning, corporate retreats, social responsibility, whole systems approaches, interdisciplinary integration, learning organizations, servant leadership, and sustainability all grew out of this field of practice in organizations, including the large multinational corporations.

While the human potential movement opened new possibilities for individual growth in people, and the organization development movement has opened new possibilities for organizations, now is the time for a new movement to create new possibilities for society as a whole. This represents a natural progression: from the individual to the organizational to the societal. All it takes is the collective will and intention of enough folks.

THE GREEN MOVEMENT

The Green Movement started in Europe, and the German Greens are generally regarded as the "mother" of all Green parties, although they are not the oldest or the first Green party to enter a national government. Their significance comes from being the first Green party to have a strong presence in the legislature of a large nation, gaining 28 seats out of 497 in the German Parliament in 1983.

Along similar "green" lines, corporate social responsibility (CSR) became a cause in the U.S. in the 1960s but received new life in the

1980s, giving rise to the formation of the Social Venture Network in 1987 and Businesses for Social Responsibility in 1992.

For the past thirty or so years, a growing number of theorists, authors, scientists, and futurists have been challenging people to looking toward a better future. This is causing people all over the world, particularly in the industrialized economies, to question evolution, and to examine the possibility of evolving consciously rather than defaulting to chance or system aberrations. Environmental sustainability has always been a key focus of the greens, and for many in the movement the wider focus includes social justice and self-actualization.

Awareness of our collective dependency on oil (a primary concern of the Green Movement) is not yet a priority in the general public's crowded attention. However, alternative fuel research, testing, and research are underway and market acceptance has begun. We can expect more as it becomes clearer to more people just how much we rely on petroleum products. This is one example of our ending the denial of dependency, confronting the truth instead of blindly going on in ignorance.

CONFLUENCE OF FORCES

So let us take a contextual overview of all these forces of transformation, those considered here and others not mentioned, and see how they have amassed over the past several decades. Recognized one at a time they may seem like simple historical milestones, but taken together they represent a rising tide of pressure to avoid the negative and attract the positive, avoid the pain and enjoy the gain.

Here is a summary of these movements, discoveries and developments in our society, listed chronologically. For those that don't have definable starting dates I've assigned my best guesses.

Social Movements, Discoveries and Developments (1770-2011)
Divine Right of Kings starts losing legitimacy (1770s)

James Watt's steam engine invented—birth of Industrial Age
    (1775)
Adam Smith publishes *The Wealth of Nations*—birth of modern
    capitalism (1776)
U.S. Declaration of Independence signed—first modern
    democracy (1776)
Common Sense published—beginning of democratic philosophy
    (1776)
Immanuel Kant publishes "What Is Enlightenment?" (1784)
U.S. Constitution signed (1789)
Social Darwinism is born as a business philosophy (1851)
Emancipation Proclamation (1863)
The birth of scientific management in factories (1911)
Corporations are tallest buildings and most dominant
    institutions (1913)
Henry Ford's popularization of mass production assembly lines
    (circa 1915)
U.S. women are granted the right to vote (1920)
General Systems Theory/systems dynamics published (1930s)
12 Step recovery programs started with founding of A.A.
    (1935)
Horror of the Holocaust discovered (1944)
Atomic bomb first used in WW II (1945), birth of the Nuclear
    Age
"Suburbanitis" begins (circa 1945)
Formation of the United Nations (1945)
Scientists create the "Doomsday Clock" (1947)
United Nations Universal Declaration of Human Rights
    (1948)
Popularity of mass market printing (1950s)
Start of widespread credit card purchasing (1950s)
U.S. Supreme Court rules school segregation unconstitutional
    (1954)

U.S. Civil Rights Act (1957)

Humanistic psychology founded (1950s)

Decline of deference to experts (started in 1955)

Television sound bites become commonplace (1960s)

Nanotechnology is born (1960s)

Blending of Eastern and Western philosophies (1960s)

Popularization of recreational drugs (1960s)

Quantum physics widely accepted (Bell's Theorem published in 1964)

U.S. passes Civil Rights Act (1964)

Human potential movement is named (1966)

Plans to flood Grand Canyon stopped (1968)

Women's movement is launched (1968)

Recognizing our interdependence; interconnectedness of humanity (1970s)

Environmental movement catches on (1970s)

Consciousness and spirituality movement is born in the U.S. (circa 1970s)

Advent of neuroscience as a distinct discipline (early 1970s)

Skinheads originate in U.K. (1970s)

The end of pure Taylorism as convention in business (1970s)

Production of the single chip microprocessor (1971)

President Nixon repeals the Bretton Woods Agreement (1971)

Founding of the Institute of Noetic Sciences (1973)

European Union formed (1973)

Short-term stock speculation becomes synonymous with "investment" (circa 1975)

First World Conference on Women, Mexico City (1975)

Birth of the microcredit movement (1976)

Driving while intoxicated becomes "illegitimate" (1980)

Personal computers become commonplace (1980s)

Rise of "opinionism" (mid-1980s to present)

Cause Marketing begins (1980s)

"Shock radio" catches on in U.S. (1980s)

Democracy becomes most popular form of governance in the world (1980s)

Internet, availability of information, *Global Brain* (1983)

Rise in complementary currencies noticed (1984)

The Caux Round Table is formed (1986)

End of the Cold War (1989)

Age Wave phenomenon (publication of the book *The Age Wave* in 1989)

Communication revolution, telegraph to Internet (1900s)

Social healing movement (started mid-1990s)

Globalization takes hold (1990s)

End of communism in USSR (1991)

Open source movement begins (1991)

Linux, the people's operating system, is given away (1991)

Businesses for Social Responsibility founded (1992)

South Africa's Truth & Reconciliation Project (1994)

"Cultural Creatives" subculture discovered by sociologist (1994)

End of apartheid in South Africa (1994)

The End of the Nation State and the dominance of the corporation (1995)

Fourth World Conference on Women, Beijing (1995)

Biomimicry breaks out as a new science (1997)

Sharp rise in U.S. personal bankruptcy filings (1997)

China shifts to socialist capitalism (building to 1999)

Rolling Stone blows whistle on "Rock-Porn Connection" (1999)

War on Terrorism is declared by U.S. President George W. Bush (2001)

Last update to the Doomsday Clock (2002)

The "flattened" world; three billion more people join the market (2004)

The Wisdom of Crowds published (2004)

Longevity revolution (underway)

Emergence of neurocardiology (underway)

Election of Barack Obama as President of the U.S. (2008)

Passage of the U.S. Troubled Asset Relief Program (2008 and still ongoing)

Pro-democracy movement beginning in Middle East and Northern Africa (2011)

As you can see, most of these new developments have occurred in the past few years, so all this wisdom has just become available, allowing us to think much differently than our fathers and mothers did. We have become somewhat used to what Paul Ray calls "re-framing" our thinking, having shifted our mindsets about women's roles, the environment, personal development, addictions, religion, social responsibility, employment, drinking and driving, psychology, and all these other late entries into our cultures. Though far from a fully comprehensive list, the forces for change I've mentioned above have made us more conscious, offered us new insights into being human, and left us more open to changing the way we think, live and work.

All that we've considered so far now leads us to the heavy lifting: global mind change. This requires delegitimizing many of our old ways of being together and creating legitimacy for some radical new ways of living together.

Chapter 8
THE NEW LEGITIMACY

One of the least appreciated powers latent in the populace is the legitimacy people give to systems and cultures, even those the people feel oppressed by or by which they are victimized. As we stand on this threshold of a Great Dream, we need a new awareness of what we are empowering and making legitimate through our actions or, more often, our failure to act.

When the Berlin Wall came down, within one day the legitimacy for that wall disappeared—for the citizens of West Germany as well as for the East German guards who might have shot anyone climbing the wall the day before. When more people recognize that powerful economic, political and military institutions persist because they have legitimacy that comes from the people, major revolutions can begin to occur. The 2011 prodemocracy movement in the Middle East and Northern Africa has served as a more current model and, like most major social transformations, it is too early to tell how it is going to turn out.

Willis Harman addresses the issue of *legitimacy* and further explains the enormous power we yield as members of the society that bestows this legitimacy. He writes:

Some of these changes have amounted to profound transformations—for instance the transition from the Roman Empire to Medieval Europe, or from the Middle Ages to modern times. Others have been more specific, such as the constitution of democratic governments in England and America, or the termination of slavery as an accepted institution.[1]

Harman's main point on this: "People give legitimacy and they can take it away." Any challenge to the established legitimacy is likely to be the "most powerful force for change to be found in history." Harman then adds another principle to go with the previous one: "By deliberately changing the internal image of reality, people can change the world. Perhaps the only limits to the human mind are those we believe in."

Swiss philosopher Jean Gebser postulates that our consciousness has evolved from "preconsciousness" to "magical consciousness" and then to "mental consciousness." Like a rainbow's spectrum of a single light beam, the single divine consciousness develops in the plurality of these forms. Theologian Willigis Jaeger writes, "We stand today on the threshold of a further level of consciousness. Our personal welfare and the continuation of our species will depend largely on whether we can successfully take that next step."[2]

History is filled with many examples of how we hold on to old ideas, of how slow many of us are to embrace new ideas, preferring the familiar to the unfamiliar, even when the unfamiliar is the truth. One example is overcoming the collective legitimacy of "miasma" as a disease theory. The miasmatic theory of disease began in the Middle Ages and continued to the mid-1800s. One proponent of the miasmatic theory was the famous Crimean War nurse, Florence Nightingale.

When miasma was the wisdom of the day, bad smells were believed to cause disease, so the cure of plagues of various sorts was to clean up anything that smelled bad, including bad breath. Centuries of legitimacy for this theory allowed millions to die before the miasmatic theory was disproved by John Snow following a cholera epidemic in the central London district of Soho in 1854. Because the theory had such prominence among Italian scientists, that country refused to believe the new findings until thirty years later.

William James reminds us that "We have to live today by what truth we can get today and be ready tomorrow to call it falsehood." History is filled with examples of yesterday's truths turning into tomorrow's falsehoods, and there is no reason why today's truths—those ideas to which we grant legitimacy—may not become unacceptable tomorrow. All we need to do is remove the legitimacy we give our ideas about how things have to be.

As I share these views about the power of shifting legitimacy, my listeners and readers often ask, "Well, John, this is all terrific stuff . . . great concepts . . . but what can we *do*? Where do we begin?" Many people insist on having tools, methodologies or techniques for action before they will allow themselves to entertain big ideas. They want to see how something will work out *before* they choose to play. This is looking for a *guarantee*—the ego's way of avoiding any game it cannot win. There is no courage in playing it safe and there are certainly no transformations possible.

The founders of the United States weren't playing it safe when they committed themselves to establishing a nation on self-evident truths. They made monarchy illegitimate and invented a new form of democracy. This had not been done before, so it certainly wasn't safe. There were no guarantees assuring them they'd succeed in their stand, their commitment, their risk. But they knew they were on to something important, a unique opportunity to create something exciting, something wanted by all people who yearned for inner and outer freedom.

A corollary to holding out for a guarantee is wanting a *formula* or plan for action. This reflects the slippery notion that Daddy or

Mommy will show me what to do—that adolescent desire to have a "prescription for doing" so responsibility for our actions can be laid off on someone else. This is also the "I was just following orders" syndrome. Either option, the guarantee or the formula, is a cop-out that avoids recognizing that we really know what needs to be done.

THE SCARCITY MINDSET

A primary example of the old legitimacy is a mindset based in scarcity and separation, which begets overconsumption as a means of being better than others. Scarcity shows up as an ongoing obsession to acquire more, trying to satisfy an insatiable appetite for something, such as love, sex, money, shoes, suits, real estate, and other possessions. Conspicuous consumption is but one symptom of this mindset made legitimate by a scarcity consciousness—the belief there isn't a sufficient amount of something so one has to take what one can while one has the opportunity.

Believing that things are scarce is a self-fulfilling prophecy. When people think from scarcity, they hoard, accumulate and acquire more than they need because they fear they might need it whenever the feared calamity occurs. Some people get carried away and become socially acceptable hoarders; we call them "collectors" but their collections are often of ridiculous proportion, exceeding legitimacy from any point of view other than that of another very wealthy person. Some nouveau riche people find they cannot stop acquiring wealth, driven largely by their memories of insufficiencies in their childhood. Thus they acquire unimaginable wealth, so much that it requires management and overseeing for its own sake, without any thought about leveling off at "enough."

History shows us examples of whole cultures that became extinct because of scarcity—early Easter Island inhabitants being one. Isolated on their island paradise in the Pacific, the natives harvested all their timber to serve their obsession with carved stone heads. Felled timber served as a means of moving these huge sculptures over the island's terrain, but no one was watching out for their deteriorating ecosystem. Eventually, the people became divided and war broke out. Archeologists' studies of this extinct culture confirm that scarcity can lead to conflict and violence which, in an isolated culture like Easter Island, can lead easily to extinction.

**Growing population + diminishing resources =
a formula for extinction.**

A sufficiency consciousness, in contrast, relieves the culture from the need to hoard, or over consume, as there is no fear of "not enough" or of "being ordinary." I know several wealthy people who, after self-examination and some consciousness raising of their own, were able to see the opulence in their lives and chose to simplify, downsizing from palatial estates to simpler homes, from multiple houses in various parts of the world to a couple, from a stable of cars to one or two. These people also realized how much effort, even worry, they had invested in maintaining their "stuff." Simplifying their lives provided a side benefit of freedom from concern and attention. The word I hear a lot from these people to describe this feeling is "liberated." Such individuals release scarcity consciousness and begin living from a context of sufficiency.

If you are looking for the means to bring about the Great Dream as you read this, I suggest you stop pretending that you don't know and own what you do know. You already know what needs doing to bring forth the Great Dream—at least your part in it. You see the problems every day. You can also see solutions, if you take some time and put some of your consciousness into the matter. Who knows better than you what needs fixing—or complete transformation—in the matters you encounter every day? Stop leaning on external authorities who might offer formulas or concepts that you will then evaluate, discount or embrace as possible practices for yourself. This is the teenage laziness we've perpetuated all these centuries.

DISTINCTIONS

Let's compare yesterday's legitimacies with tomorrow's. Here are a few distinctions I can offer:

> The existing or old legitimacies are based on "fixer-upper" thinking, linear approaches to problems, wanting very predictable outcomes. The context is based in fear, insecurity, mistrust, separation, rankism, and fundamentalism. It breeds addictions, violence, lack of intimacy and incivility.
>
> The new legitimacy we can create if we so choose is based on a systemic redesign of society, and on trust, love, connection, civility and wholism. It then generates compassion, reconciliation, understanding, dignitarianism, and a spirit-centered reality.

The closest thing I've seen to this new legitimacy in the world is the "*ubuntu*" approach to transformation used in South Africa, which is based upon our existence and our humanness being reliant on each others' humanity. This consciousness says that if I hurt you, I am hurting myself. If I dehumanize you, I am dehumanizing myself. Largely due to this legitimacy, South Africa ended apartheid by reconciliation rather than civil war.

Distinctions Between Existing and New Legitimacies

Existing Legitimacies	New Legitimacies
Nationalism	Globalism
War is inevitable	War is unacceptable
Looking out for #1; me first	Everyone's basic needs are met
Reality = parts making up a whole	Spaceship Earth, wholism
Physical, material domain is dominant	All domains respected equally
Economics rule	Holism of all systems
Dominate nature and others, force over	Having dominion, mastery without force
Patriarchy dominates	Masculine and feminine in partnership

Existing Legitimacies	New Legitimacies
Cause-effect, linear thinking	Systems dynamics
Separatism	Interconnectivity
Form-focused	Appreciation of context
Adolescent	Adult
Fear-driven	Caring, loving
Short-term payoffs	Long-term sustainability
External gratification	Internal satisfaction
Discussion, debate, one-upsmanship	Dialogue, inquiry
Resignation, vengeance, retribution	Reconciliation, forgiveness
Holding positions	Taking a stand
Fundamentalism of all kinds	Natural knowing of context
Scarcity; there's never enough	Sufficiency
Dogma-based worship	Direct-knowing devotion
Clever manipulation, coercion	Free market choices
Privileged advantage	Fairness
Rampant rankism	Dignitarian culture
Suspiciousness, mistrust	Trust
Tyranny, oppression	Self-government, personal responsibility
Winning by beating others	Winning in "cooperative competition"
I- It (Buber)	I- Thou (Buber)
Desperation and fear influencing choices	True freedom of choice

THE POWER OF TAKING A STAND

In my last book, *Getting to the Better Future*, I quote global thinker and philanthropist Lynne Twist on the subject of taking a stand. She says, "Taking a stand is a way of living and being that draws on a place within yourself that is at the very heart of who you are. When you take a stand, you find your place in the universe, and you have the capacity to move the world."[3]

Twist also talks about living "the committed life" and lives her own life from that place of commitment, inspiring anyone who is fortunate enough to know her.

Other examples of individuals with a committed stand include John Robbins, heir to the Baskin Robbins fortune. This courageous man turned his back on his inheritance because he refused to continue supporting a world of pollution and extinctions. Instead, he chose to "actively engage with the living world." Julia Butterfly Hill took a stand by sitting in a tree for 738 days, 180 feet high in the canopy of an ancient redwood, to help make the world aware of the plight of our ancestral forests. Mahatma Gandhi, Mother Teresa and Martin Luther King, Jr., took stands for what they believed. So did Apple Computer founders Steve Jobs and Steve Wozniak, MADD (Mothers Against Drunk Driving) founder Candace Lightner, Nelson Mandela, and Mikhail Gorbachev. All serve as examples of what one person can do when they take a stand for something they really believe in.

And who can forget the television image of the young man standing in front of a column of Chinese army tanks during the Tiananmen Square democracy demonstrations in 1989?

As the lead tank altered its path to avoid the young student, the man calmly shifted sideways so he remained in its path. Nicknamed

Famous photo of "tank man" during Tiananmen Square pro-democracy demonstrations in 1989. *AP photo, used with permission*

"Tank Man," his stand was clear from the camera's perspective, and inspired millions around the world.

How about the collective stand taken by hundreds of thousands—perhaps millions—of Arabs in the prodemocracy movement sweeping through the Middle East and Africa more recently?

Stand-taking requires courage. Paul Mlotok, formerly the top-ranked oil industry analyst on Wall Street, says, "courage can be as important as the choice." Taking a stand requires a kind of "spiritual bravery" that comes from one's soul—not a war-hero type of bravado. The courage in taking the stand can sometimes be just as big a factor in one's life as the stand itself.

Mlotok quotes the Hindu avatar Krishna: "A warrior who has acquired great merit, and who has such an opportunity for battle, is like a person who has found a wish-fulfilling gem in his path." Mlotok elaborates, "[F]acing difficult choices is not just something to be endured, but rather a blessing for which we should be thankful. It is a chance to 'do battle'—to develop our spiritual skills and understanding."[4]

There are thousands of stories of people who have taken stands throughout history. We can all recall those who inspired us in some way. Stands are different from positions. Stands provide inspiration that generates more stand-taking and action by others. Positions, on the other hand, largely invite polarization, either opposition or agreement, which fosters more debate, conflict and sometimes violence.

STAND-TAKING AS A WAY OF LIFE

Former Fetzer Winery CEO and organic wine farmer Paul Dolan tells us that once you take a stand *as an organization*, shifts in corporate culture start to happen. This is a higher personal commitment, affecting a company and ultimately an entire industry. He says:

> First, a stand is personal for each of us. It's about see-
> ing a personal possibility of making a contribution

and fully expressing our commitment to that. When I think about our stand on organic viti-culture, it connects me to my immediate, personal desire to make a difference, right here, right now, in behalf of the earth.

Second, each of us is responsible for its completion. We don't have a part in the play, we are the play. Everyone is the source of the stand, not just a resource to it. Each of us is responsible for finding new opportunities, new solutions, new ways forward.

Third, each of us is responsible for generating the conversation about the stand. This grows naturally out of the first two dimensions. You're responsible for making the stand come alive for others, to attract them to it as a possibility, and to advance its discovery and exploration.[5]

Entrepreneurs and business leaders like Dolan who commit themselves to their visions are experienced stand-takers. Their courage in holding to their visions and not allowing them to be hijacked is as important to their soul as it is to the vision to which they've committed themselves. They know how to maintain their vision and their resonance so they are undeterred no matter what distractions come their way.

The world is in great need of stand-takers right now, particularly in our organizations. Most importantly, they are needed in those large, publicly traded corporations. Many, many people inside these companies know what needs doing. The Wall Street culture leading up to 2009 and the companies involved in the scandals presented many opportunities for individuals to take stands when they saw something of questionable integrity going past their desk. But almost all remained silent, choosing not to be whistleblowers and instead "going along."

Conspiracies of silence are just as complicit. Martin Luther King, Jr. says, "Our lives begin to end the day we become silent about things that matter." People who remain silent lose part of themselves; their aliveness takes a hit. King also tells us, "A time comes when silence is betrayal." It is betrayal of ourselves as well as of the stand one might have taken.

We don't need more answers to our problems. We have plenty of answers. What we lack is enough people willing to take courageous stands—to act on what they already know. Many people pretend they don't know, but down deep they do.

When confronted with taking a stand, the egoic mind tends to manufacture instant rationale for inertia. "What can I do, I'm only one person?" is a common one. "I'm not in a position to make any real difference" is another. I love a saying I first heard from business entrepreneur and social activist Anita Roddick: "If you ever think you are too small to make a difference, try getting into a sleeping bag with a mosquito."

Historian Alan John Percivale Taylor reminds us that "All change in history, all advance, comes from the non-conformists. If there had been no troublemakers, no dissenters, no whistleblowers, we should still be living in caves."

PARADIGM CHANGES: WHAT THEY ARE AND HOW THEY HAPPEN

We frequently hear references these days to "paradigm change" and "old versus new paradigms." Ironically, there was a time in the late 1980s when colleagues of mine would scoff at this highbrow word borrowed from academe, believing it could never become part of the parlance of business. No one could have predicted how popular the term would become.

Michael Ray, Stanford School of Business Professor Emeritus, was using the term when he launched a course initially called "New

Paradigm Business" at the Palo Alto campus in the 1980s. Just a few years later, I heard middle managers for a phone company talking amongst themselves after a business conference, freely using the terms "old paradigm" to describe people they knew whose ideas were outmoded, and "new paradigm" to portray their own "more enlightened" perspective. This gave me pause, seeing how this new term could be cheapened through misuse and misunderstanding.

Thomas Kuhn is widely cited as the first person to popularize the term "paradigm" in his book *The Structure of Scientific Revolutions*. Kuhn held posts as a Professor of Philosophy and History of Science at Princeton, MIT, and Harvard. Before he died, it was rumored that he regretted having used the term due to its prominent misuse. According to futurist Walter Truett Anderson, in his book *Reality Isn't What It Used to Be*:

> Kuhn was a major step toward a postmodern view of science . . . [he] offered a different view of how scientific progress takes place: he said scientists do not make their progress by adding one fact to another in a mechanistic, objective sort of way, but rather lurch ahead from time to time in sudden creative bursts he called paradigm shifts.

He quotes Kuhn as saying:

> [B]elief systems never quite manage to explain all the facts. Researchers keep coming across anomalies, findings the prevailing theory can't account for. But for a while the theory prevails anyway (partly because some researchers ignore findings that don't fit it), and as research proceeds, more anomalies accumulate. Eventually somebody comes up with a new explanatory system that replaces the old one.[6]

Anderson himself defines paradigm as "a social construction of reality, a belief system that prevails in a certain scientific community." Harman's definition is: "the basic way of perceiving, thinking, valuing, and doing associated with a particular vision of reality."

Elaborating, Anderson tells us that Kuhn defined major scientific paradigm shifts as leaps into new cognitive patterns or different worldviews. Again quoting Kuhn:

> When paradigms change, the world itself changes with them. Led by a new paradigm, scientists adopt new instruments and look in new places. Even more important, during revolutions scientists see new and different things when looking with familiar instruments in places they have looked before. It is rather as if the professional community had been suddenly transported to another planet where familiar objects are seen in a different light and are joined by unfamiliar ones as well.[7]

Of course, Kuhn was discussing paradigm changes in science. But the same dynamics apply when addressing paradigm changes in how we think about our reality—how it needs to be; what's possible; and what limits we put ourselves under when we are heavily invested in our worldviews or mental models.

Anderson writes:

> In Kuhn's account, paradigm shifts are social, not individual: there is no such thing as a paradigm without a community. Paradigm shifts take place within communities, and sometimes help create them: by adopting a paradigm, a loosely constituted network of scholars may begin to turn into a profession or a discipline.[8]

ABOUT CHANGE OF STATE

Paradigm shifts normally occur after a certain number of people have a change of consciousness—what some may call a "change of state." Let me insert a few thoughts from the evolutionists' perspective. David Kyle, a consultant and a fellow faculty member of the Center for Leadership Studies in the summer of 2005, once referenced a paper he had presented earlier at Yale on "causality consciousness." Kyle noted that when a paradigm shift is pending, preparing to take that evolutionary leap, there is often a "bunching up" of the species or particles or whatever is preparing to make the leap, and they collect around a threshold. Kyle says that change of state is different from "evolutionary adaptation" as we normally think of it. In his Yale paper he writes, "Change of state for any species is that point where the entire species faces an evolutionary jump toward a radical and unpredictable next step in its evolution." He contends that:

> Either the entire species jumps across the chasm together, or the species flames out and dies trying to change. This means the species doesn't "dribble" across a threshold. Either the whole group goes through the transformation or they die out together, as so many species have done over the history of this planet.[9]

In addressing the potential extinction of humanity, Kyle offers a passage I find quite sobering,: "The most critical condition for change of state to happen is the presence of environmental conditions that could actually cause the extinction of the entire species."[10]

This threat cannot be illusionary. It must be real. The entire species must face potential extinction to catalyze the shift. Homo sapiens have not faced the threat of total species extinction by their own hand until the atomic bomb emerged in the mid-twentieth century. It is this pressure of total extinction that brings about the state change of complexity-consciousness, thus drawing the species forward in the evolutionary process.

Kyle concurs with Barbara Marx Hubbard, who points to shifts in consciousness running parallel with evolutionary shifts. He writes, "At each change of state there is an inward movement in the development of consciousness, away from the pull toward more outward complexity . . . a tension between complexity and consciousness generates energy to create the transformation." This creative tension works for the entire species, not merely at the individual or organizational levels.

LIVING AND WORKING BETWEEN PARADIGMS

The sigmoid curves I introduced in chapter 4 represent paradigm changes. The graphic below shows an established paradigm starting to lose legitimacy while something new is being conceived. As the old fades, the new takes hold. But the gap or cleavage between the two paradigms represents a period of uncertainty, which often makes people very nervous. Sometimes they are so fearful that they fight off the new paradigm and do their best to cling to the old, much like a person clinging to a flotation device in the ocean.

One of the seldom discussed and rarely realized phenomena about shifting paradigms is that when a person is immersed within the existing paradigm he or she cannot see or even imagine how things might be in a new one. When such a transformation does occur, it is often seen as a "miracle" because it wasn't consciously envisioned by many people. But a few who can envision how things could be different can shape the process.

Paradigm changes have historically been born out of some radical, sometimes off-the-wall theories, while the rest of the world remained firmly set in a previously adapted paradigm. An example frequently used in science is the Copernican Revolution: prior to the realization that the Earth revolved around the Sun, civilization and the church deemed the reality to be the exact opposite. A more

Ending of One Paradigm and Birthing of a New One

The diagram above is one I often draw during my talks. While the <u>existing paradigm</u> starts losing legitimacy, a **new paradigm** is usually being born. The new notion arises as the old one withers. What bothers most people who live through these transitions is the gap or chasm between paradigms, where the old is failing and the new one hasn't caught hold yet. This can be a time of seeming chaos, uncertainty and, for many, great insecurity.

recent example of a paradigm shift took place in California's Silicon Valley when the idea of a "personal computer" was born. Some paradigm changes take centuries to gain legitimacy with the masses, some take only decades.

We are presently in the midst of a major paradigm shift in the way we human beings think: the way we think about each other, the way we think about how the world works, and the way we relate to one another. In other words, the way we experience reality. Not *what* we think about but *how* we think. As we mentioned above, when paradigms change there is a period when the older one is losing credibility and legitimacy while a new one is being born. As the existing well-entrenched paradigm begins falling off in acceptance, the new one is gaining legitimacy with growing numbers of the population.

Today, paradigm shifts need not take centuries, as many have throughout history. The length of time between one paradigm losing credibility entirely and the new one being completely accepted can vary, depending upon how readily people let go of the old and adopt the new. This is where understanding what's going on can facilitate more rapid adoption. After all, when you understand the nature of the changes underway you will be less inclined to fear the process, more trusting and allowing of the new to be birthed. Instead of resisting the emerging paradigm, people can become "midwives," ushering it in under more welcome circumstances.

As I noted at the beginning of this chapter, my favorite example of a rapid paradigm shift is when the legitimacy of the Berlin Wall disappeared almost overnight in the late 1980s. Naturally there were many factors building up to it, but when it was time for it to go, everyone knew it. Even the young East German guards who a day earlier might have fired upon those mounting the Wall to tear it down knew it was time for this monument to go.

When one's consciousness or thinking is tied to the paradigm that is losing legitimacy, one might panic, like when one is riding a roller coaster that starts its rapid fall after cresting at its peak. After all, the established paradigm is what we have been living in for some time. It is familiar territory. We have learned how to function in it and how it works. We may have even developed some expertise in dealing with this paradigm, so we are used to it and have a huge reliance on it.

In contrast, the new paradigm is completely unknown—unfamiliar and untested. No one has developed any mastery over it yet. Therefore, embracing a new paradigm can be very scary. Parts of the old paradigm may still apply in the new, but we don't know *which* ones. Some things we learned in the past we will need to unlearn. But *what things*, we do not yet know.

Compare the way we think, our belief system, to the operating system in your computer. It makes a huge difference which operating system runs your computer, since all of its programs and other functions are based upon the underlying system. Similarly, it makes a huge difference which "operating system" we use in the way we think. To continue the analogy, it makes a huge difference whether the system architecture is open or closed.

Sometimes our operating system is irreversibly contaminated from within itself. We may have moments of realization—even powerful transcendent experiences when we suspend our thinking, like taking a short holiday from it—but so often we return to the primary operating system. In other words, sometimes we can temporarily override the operating system—get out of our minds—but we are rarely able to transcend it permanently.

I see this in my own life all too frequently. I have a peak experience and feel wonderful. I see joy and love as the true reality and recognize huge possibilities for us all as enlightened human beings, consciously evolving to exciting new levels of freedom with responsibility. Then I reengage the world and all the systemic forces that accompany living and working in the present day consensus reality. I sometimes go back to sleep, going about my familiar routines, and before I know it I'm back in the old mindset, which is based upon separation, scarcity and fear. My transcendent experience becomes a mere memory, like a holiday vacation rather than a new way of living my life.

Transcending the old paradigm—truly living moment to moment in the new one—requires us to give up something we might think of as very precious. This treasured attachment is the way we have been thinking all our lives, the old operating system. Thinking dominates our lives—the way we live together, the way we work, and the way we relate to one another. As we've pointed out throughout this book, the operating system for this thinking to which we're so attached is based upon a context of fear, scarcity, materialism and separateness. As a result, all choices, behaviors and attitudes that we hold are strongly influenced by this context. This is the old paradigm.

Mystics and philosophers have told us for centuries that love is an absolute truth, a context for life on Earth, and that balance in our lives requires equal emphasis on both the material and spiritual. The founders of these United States applied this wisdom when they started a nation built on freedom to pursue material wealth as well as spiritual enlightenment. Social scientists tell us that there are ways for all of us to live together and have sufficient resources for every-one's basic needs. Modern-day physical scientists have demonstrat-ed that we are indeed all connected, at a molecular and resonance level—all part of one whole. Yet, our old thinking refuses to accept this wisdom. Despite the evidence, we hold on for dear life to our outdated core beliefs and act accordingly every day, even though this worldview results in much unnecessary suffering and pain.

How do we give this up? How do we let go of such deep-seated thinking? Continuing the computer analogy, we need to replace the operating system. Einstein said it: "Everything has changed save our modes of thinking, and we thus drift towards unparalleled catas-trophes." The present system of thought is truly outmoded. While people may be familiar with Einstein's warning, we live each day as if he was either stupid or completely wrong. Closer to the truth . . . people may simply not know what he meant by another "mode of thinking."

MIDWIFING THE NEW, HOSPICING THE OLD

I don't have the blueprint for the new operating system, but I can read the signs. I see obvious requirements for consciously growing up, I see new principles that may apply. These include being in dialogue with one another; not another type of intellectual discussion or social conversation, but true dialogue. Another would be appreciating the nonphysical senses that we in the West may not be familiar with any longer. Some of these lost senses—call them "sixth" or "seventh" senses—are quite natural. Animals and indigenous people can sense things we can't. Our senses for resonance, texture and subtle energies of all sorts have been deferred to the five physical senses over the centuries.

Still another aspect of this new operating system would include accepting a direct relationship with a higher power, not a religious fundamentalism steeped in "One and Only Truth," but rich, comfort-able spiritual partnerships with whatever we call that "power greater than ourselves." Within this new paradigm we would be learning new things—like what science is telling us *now*—not simply relying upon what we learned in school decades ago. We can learn how to be more comfortable with paradox, without compulsively seeking to reconcile seeming contradictions; we can become more willing to live with questions. We can allow for a balance with both the masculine and feminine, so that integrated partnership can exist in our collective approach to relating to one another in the world.

At times, I have struggled with my own thinking, finding myself straddling the two paradigms as if I have one foot on the dock and the other in an untied boat alongside. In times of challenge and stress, my habitual default has been to rely on the old system even though I know it's outmoded. I long to rely on the new paradigm, to trust it completely and engage all those fears and other emotions in their full intensity. More often than I wish, however, I end up resorting to or intellectually grasping the old familiar paradigm in desperation when it looks too scary and unfamiliar to rely on the new one.

A Course of Love states: "You can be faithful to but one thought system. One is the thought system of separated self and is based upon separation. The other is the thought system of creation and is based on union."[11] When I attempt to straddle or hop back and forth between these thought systems—these two paradigms—I become drained of energy, ineffective in both of them, and reenslaved by my ego.

On a societal level, many people are being challenged with this same straddle. If more people recognized this interim "between-ness" as a transition to a more appropriate paradigm for advanced human evolution, there would be less trepidation about this valley of uncertainty. Instead of fighting to maintain and shore up the old paradigm, there would be more embracing of the new. Instead of resisting, there would be more people helping to birth the new system, the new context, the new paradigm. It is a time to let go of the old outmoded ways of being so we can take the next step in fulfilling our true potential. After all, this is hardly the peak for human development on Earth.

Can we achieve this transcendent shift to a new paradigm? Can we do so relatively soon, before the straddling becomes unbearable? Will the shift, once completed, allow us to create the better future that is eluding us right now? To all these questions I answer a hearty YES.

And, perhaps this is where a warning might be in order. Years ago I learned that humans tend to make the old ways "wrong" and "bad" in order to elevate their new habits, jobs or relationships. You see this happen when people move to a different city, get divorced, change careers and so forth. We justify our decisions. This could happen as we shift from old legitimacies to new ones better suited to our times. I strongly suggest that we all treat the old ways, the old legitimacies that have supported us in evolving to this point, the tried and true mindsets that have allowed us to grow this far, as stepping stones in our development as a society. I suggest we don't suddenly switch allegiances and start badmouthing the old and proselytizing the new, beating people over the head with our righteousness.

Conversely, let us advance the new with some sensitivity, like giving birth to a new baby. One friend of mine introduced me to the idea of "midwifing" the new legitimacy, a process perhaps more familiar to women than to men, but nonetheless graspable in its meaning. She said that as society makes this transition, we need midwives of the new legitimacy to come into being, while simultaneously we "hospice" the old, being respectful of how it has served us to this point in our history. Both midwifery and hospice care require a compassionate approach to the task before us as we set out to cocreate our future together.

MORE WISE WORDS

We're nearing the end of this adventuresome consideration, and it seems like time for a review of what has proceeded. We've revisited the original vision set out by the founders of the United States of

America, and recontextualized it for the entire world in the twenty-first century. We've examined our achievements and progression as humans, especially very recent discoveries and developments that weren't available to earlier societies.

Besides appreciating these new resources, we've also reviewed our new awareness and learnings, not only explicit knowledge but the intrinsic consciousness that allows us to see things differently. We've also looked at our darker sides, our collective "shadow," the ways we sabotage change and frustrate efforts to transcend the status quo and improve our world substantially. We've addressed how the mind, our individual and collective consciousness, can be either our best ally or our worst enemy in achieving what we claim we want.

Now we have all the resources we need to create the kind of world we want and everything we need to know. The only thing left is whether or not we have the will and the courage to take our stands for this better future we have envisioned.

I'm moved here to quote an old sage from early twentieth-century America, Samuel Clemens, alias Mark Twain, who wrote:

> Twenty years from now you will be more disappointed by the things you didn't do than by the ones you did do. So throw off the bowlines. Sail away from the safe harbor. Catch the trade winds in your sails. Explore. Dream. Discover.

We've heard from many wise people in earlier pages that "Something new is happening. And it has to do with *it all*—the whole," as Peter Senge wrote. Whether it is James Surowiecki telling us that "[W]e've been programmed to be collectively smart" or Peter Drucker counseling us that "The best way to determine the future is to create it," it is clear that we are in charge. And international futurist-consultant Adam Kahane reminds us of something we know down deep already:

Every one of us gets to choose, in every encounter every day, which world we will contribute to bringing into reality. When we chose the closed way, we participate in creating a world filled with force and fear. When we choose an open way, we participate in creating another, better world.[12]

Georg Simmel too reminds us that we have a choice as to what kind of society we want to be. Willis Harman points to the power we have: "A challenge to legitimacy is probably the most powerful force for change to be found in history ... people can withhold legitimacy, and thus change the world ..." And Bernard Lietaer says, "[F]or the first time in human history we have available the production technologies to create unprecedented abundance."

Chapter 9
LET IT BEGIN WITH ME

This phase in our human evolution could be compared to what A.A. calls "bottoming out"—referring to the situation where the alcoholic finds himself or herself at such a low point that enough resolve is generated to do what is necessary to achieve sobriety. A.A. talks about "high bottoms" and "low bottoms," meaning that some people really hit the skids (losing their jobs, their marriages, living on the street, etc.) before they see the light while others may suffer significantly fewer consequences, perhaps simply by a breakup with someone they were dating, or some frank comments made to them by someone they respect. In either case, low bottom or high, a certain amount of shame must be experienced, usually after perpetually denying or avoiding that there's a problem.

Most recovering alcoholics agree that their lives really take off after they get sober. Once they achieve sobriety they replace alcohol as their primary relationship and establish a relationship with some form of higher power. You might say they are able to become whole as a result of hitting this bottom. Many of them actually view their recovery as a blessing, a "return to God," as some describe it.

HITTING BOTTOM OR COMING HOME?

The subtitle to *Getting to the Better Future*, my last nonfiction book, is *A Matter of Conscious Choosing*. At the risk of oversimplifying, it really does come down to how and what we choose. That freedom always lies within us. The only one who can take this freedom away from me is myself, or as the cartoon character Pogo stated so poetically several decades ago, "We have met the enemy and he is us."

Perhaps we humans are at a point of bottoming out of our addiction to our thinking, our proneness to reverting to our minds as default, and the way we think when we go there. The system we have all been enabling, that outmoded one Einstein spoke about , may be about to file a sort of "spiritual bankruptcy." While the system has been insolvent for some time, declaring it formally so may be the bottom we need to hit as a society. We can then end the denial and face the reality that our rational, industrial, scientific and adolescent mindsets have taken us as far as they can, and that it could well be time to partner with a power greater than our minds.

Peter Kingsley writes:

> Human existence is nothing but the divine life un-lived. And to start to live it, you have to come aside while you still can. You have to find the sacred spot where teacher meets disciple and the real learning begins—a learning that has nothing otherworldly about it. In actual fact it's not so much a process of learning as a stripping away of all the teaching you have ever had until you are left quite naked, facing something far greater than yourself.[1]

Kingsley's words are influenced by the ancient Greek wisdom of Socrates, Parmenides and Empedocles, yet tie so nicely into what drunks seeking sobriety told us half a century ago when they founded A.A. Allowing our previous learning to be "stripped away," to be "naked" facing Presence, opens the door to wholeness, direct experience and genuine power. Kingsley continues:

> From then on, life without the teacher is impossible anymore; unbearable; inconceivable. And there are no approximations to this unending relationship, no near hits or near misses. Either you come aside or you don't. There is no half in, half out, no voyeurism, and absolutely no bargaining. You either accept the terms you are offered or had better leave. For, as we will soon see, tricks and devices exist to make sure that those who insist on laying down their own conditions will end up staying far away.
>
> So there is a warning . . . The warning is that, until you experience your total powerlessness, you will never discover your real power.[2]

The first five words of the First Step of A.A.'s 12 Steps are, "We admitted we were powerless." Getting sober starts with this admission and, as any A.A. member with some time sober can tell you, it is the path to "real power," as Kingsley writes. The path to real power is through experiencing our powerlessness in going it alone.

This is our homecoming, a return to the place within ourselves that is the embodiment of real power—not artificial power or force over others, but authentic dominion to create bold realities. This could be what we are becoming. Michael Dowd reminds us, "We as a species are coming to our senses, and returning home to our true Self."[3]

Similar to the soul-searching an addict goes through when he or she confronts their addiction, we might want to be brutally honest about what we are becoming as the human race. We are becoming frightened, collectively addicted, personally isolated fundamentalists who have been avoiding growing up and committing ourselves to living together in harmony.

In many respects, this paradigm shift that humanity is going through is a form of "coming home." We have gone as far as we could go in relying entirely on our rational thinking, and our minds have done quite well . . . considering their limitations. But, we are humans and we have higher connections. Whether you call it "Providence"—as America's founders did—or "Higher Power," as A.A. does, or "God," as many others refer to this higher connection, it is like home to us. We are back in the womb of the Divine, completely mature and fully functioning, filled with inner wisdom and capability, yet trusting in the existence of forces beyond the human mind that we will never completely understand.

In an ironic twist . . . a paradox . . . we can find our way home to our higher connection only by bottoming out. We surrender the idea that we must have control, the illusion we are in control, and allow Divine presence to bless us, to give grace to our lives, and consciousness to our species.

Coming home involves surrender, to be sure. Not in that hang-your-head-low, prisoner-of-war way, but in a standing tall way. There is no shame in this surrender. It means abandoning our fruitless hopping along on one leg and accepting the support of a higher form of ourselves. This higher form has been standing alongside us all this time, offering us our other leg so we can stand without all the effort involved in balancing on only one. Coming home therefore means delight and celebration, returning to being fully integrated human beings.

This spiritual homecoming is also a human homecoming since we humans are as much spiritual beings as we are physical. We are a package that includes both, and when we become whole again, fully integrated as complete human beings, we have returned to our true home.

WHAT'S IT ALL MEAN?

Everything I've written to this point can be viewed as interesting, informative, conceptual brain fodder for those ever-gluttonous minds of ours, but ultimately it has to be put to use. Otherwise, what's the point?

What are you going to do with all this? Most of you will probably add it to your inner libraries, cataloged under "interesting" or "maybe someday." A few of you may feel moved to be more proactive. The choice is highly personal.

Some people would rather be part of the advance team making the path. Others prefer to wait until the way is paved, perhaps even landscaped. Some of us like to be the pathfinders in one area—say in business—but are more passive in other areas of our lives, like sports. Different people have different appetites for initiation, risk, exploring new territory and trying new things.

Most people in this world are observers who watch risk takers, trend setters and pathfinders blaze new trails, whether it is in business, fashion, sports or entertainment. That's why stadiums are built to accommodate tens of thousands of spectators while a few dozen people put on the show.

Whether to play or to watch is a personal choice each one of us makes, probably several times a day. In the case of working toward a better world, a better future for everyone, it either grabs you or it doesn't. If it still seems like folly to you, then there's no sense getting involved. Your heart won't be in it anyway.

If you are intrigued, or left wondering, then I encourage you to satisfy those wonderings and look into whatever has struck a chord with you. But dig until you have resolution. Once you have resolution, you can choose: either it is nonsense or it is possibility. It's your call. If you judge this invitation to the Great Growing Up to be nonsensical, you join the others who believe it is folly and choose not to get involved. As I said, your heart won't be in it anyway. But could you do me a favor? Please stop adding legitimacy to systems, institutions and people you aren't happy with. Then, even if you aren't choosing to be get proactively engaged in bringing forth this new paradigm, at least you will be able to live with yourself in greater integrity, knowing that you're not giving away your personal power to the very things you oppose!

If you think there is real possibility here, that we really have a shot at creating a better world and evolving ourselves consciously, then you have another choice: to play or to watch. If you choose to play, pick a place to start. It might be in your office, neighborhood, or school system; in local politics, in community action groups; with social justice issues. Get involved in shifting the consciousness about any system you select so that it becomes either obsolete—and is replaced with a better functioning one—or undergoes major surgery so it functions much closer to what is wanted from it. Avoid the palliatives and consolations. Don't compromise with superficial changes that won't make any long-term difference. Insist on real change.

If you choose to watch, just tell the truth about it. Sports fans observe. They don't play but they enjoy watching. You can be a fan of those who *are* playing the game. Like sports enthusiasts, you can be a casual observer or even a fanatic. Applying this in our consciousness game, you can read about what is going on that could change the future. You can cheer on those who are writing books, teaching systems change, trying to bring about reforms in all kinds of arenas. You can pay for your seat in this arena by contributing to causes that you support. These players can use all the support they can get. And, you can stop giving your power away to dysfunctional systems.

If you choose to be on the team of people working toward manifesting the Great Dream, then there is some work to do beyond simply shifting your mindset. And beware, your ego mind will put up all sorts of objections and reasons why this isn't going to work and why you'd be better off devoting your energies to other activities. Among the popular and paralyzing laments our minds like to offer are, "Where do I begin?" or "What can I do?" I say *grow where you are planted*. You are already more knowledgeable and skilled in those systems to which you belong and with which you are already familiar. If you feel called to bring about transformation, start where you are.

In the many years I've been at this work I constantly run into people who refuse to start doing anything until they know the "how"—the formula, the model, the technique. I love the title of consultant Peter Block's book: *The Answer to How Is Yes*. Stop spending valuable time wondering how and jump in with the rest of us, inventing as we go. Sign yourself up for bringing about the changes you know need to be made.

Whether you opt in and suit up for the Great Dream game, or merely watch how it unfolds as a spectator, it helps to know the energetic commitment of the stand you are taking. Will you play or watch aggressively or passively? If your stand is to become a leader and put yourself on the line, great! If your stand is to do nothing and hope others take the leadership roles, then that is good to know. Whatever it is, clarify your stand, for yourself. This is where you begin.

EMBODYING THE GREAT DREAM

Creating a world that works for everyone will not happen out of concentrated task mastery—like the mastery necessary in building a house or developing new software. The Great Dream will be created by lots of people sharing a dream, owning a vision, and then taking responsibility for whatever aspect of the dream they are able and willing to embody. The possibility for the Great Dream lives within each person. With deep embodiment, action will naturally follow. These actions will not be those of someone extrinsically committed to a goal, but the actions of someone really clear about what they want. These actions will not be those of someone afraid of ridicule or seeking approval. They will come naturally out of a people who possess a profound sense of freedom, yet hold themselves responsible for the world they live in. These actions will not be generated by willpower alone, but rather within the field of a will that transcends personality and includes everyone, even the Divine.

Mel Toomey talks about this in his organizational leadership program when he teaches about creating breakthroughs. He says,

"Keeping possibilities in existence until their relationships are clear leads to breakthroughs."[4] Holding "possibilities in existence" is what we do with this Great Dream. This creative tension adds legitimacy for this kind of breakthrough by deconstructing the walls of resignation and cynicism.

As I write this, I feel barely adequate in expressing myself. While I am so certain about the "ground of being" we can cocreate for ourselves, still I doubt my ability to clearly describe it. This is part of the new legitimacy I mentioned earlier. It includes knowing that some things are "unknowable" in the traditional sense, and are, therefore, ineffable. It includes our being able to get the gestalt of something without having it described in great detail or precisely blueprinted. These new senses are valued increasingly as we all learn together how to be more skilled and sensitive to subtle energies.

Most of us in the West are used to a very masculine way of operating in the world, most usually resorting to domination or manipulation to get things done. It is the way we've been taught to get results in the physical world. But it has its downsides. For example, there was a time when we took great pride in dominating nature (as if we really could). This somewhat arrogant attitude grew from so much technological success, building engineering marvels all over the world. But what is called for in creating the Great Dream is dominion, not domination, a different sort of mastery. Dominion is mastery without slaves. It is mastery without hierarchy. It is creation from within, not only from our "doing-ness" but also from our "being-ness" or personhood. This is what I'm attempting to call forth for us now.

This is how we "hold" the Great Dream, not as a procedure or a map, not as a formula or recipe, but as a shared dream with millions of facets, cocreated to serve everyone, each of whom will naturally have a different perspective or point of view. We hold it without grasping it. We have dominion of our reality without trying to dominate it, without clever maneuvering or seduction or political haggling. Embodying the Great Dream in this way we have elegant mastery without resorting to manipulative control or imposition. Could this be challenging? You bet! But it starts with taking a stand for it.

Years ago, I had a lunch conversation with Peter Senge which has stuck with me. He candidly said that personal mastery included the ability to stand in one's vision and maintain the tension, not settle for or sell out for the promised comfort of lowering one's vision. I have found this off the cuff definition to be incredibly helpful.

In the early pages of *Critical Path*, Bucky Fuller states unequivocally that "The world now has an option to become comprehensively and sustainingly successful—for all" and dedicates the entire book to describing what we need to do to achieve this. Keeping in mind that he wrote this book in the late 1970s, we are seriously behind in implementing any of his solutions nearly two generations later. Given the way we think, those who seek ideals will continue to become disappointed, perpetuating cynicism. But, as Bucky points out, we now have an option—to think differently!

Kazuo Inamori is a Japanese businessman who founded two successful companies, as well as a charitable foundation, and established the Kyoto Prize. He has a visionary perspective on a new civilization. He writes:

> [W]e can shift from growth to maturity, from competition to coexistence, and walk the path of harmony. As we traverse this path, we will witness the birth of a new civilization that is motivated by the virtue of selfless service to others. The driving force behind our current civilization is the desire for more: more leisure, more food, more money. In contrast, the new civilization will be based on love and consideration for others, the desire to help others grow and make them happy.
>
> . . . I don't know exactly what form this civilization will take or what its contents will be. Perhaps it is just a pipe dream. But I am convinced that it is not

the creation of this new civilization that is important but rather the daily effort we make to build it. It
is the process of getting there, not being there, that
refines our souls. If we elevate our minds by striv-
ing to create a new, more loving civilization, I believe
that the path to a service-oriented society will be far
shorter than we ever imagined.[5]

Another Japanese business visionary was the late Ryuzaburo
Kaku, then chair of Canon, Inc. In 1997 he wrote:

Because . . . multibillion-dollar corporations control
vast resources around the globe, employ millions of
people, and create and own incredible wealth, they
hold the future of the planet in their hands. Although
governments and individuals need to do their part,
they do not possess the same degree of wealth and
power . . . If corporations run their businesses with
the sole aim of gaining more market share or earning
more profits, they may well lead the world into economic, environmental and social ruin . . . It is our obligation as business leaders to join together to build a
foundation for world peace and prosperity.[6]

SOME THINGS TO DO AND WAYS TO BE

Bernard Lietaer proposes that "we choose to develop money systems
that will enable us to attain sustainability and community healing on
a local and global scale. These objectives are in our grasp within less
than one generation's time. Whether we materialize them or not will
depend on our capacity to cooperate with each other to consciously
reinvent our money."[7]

Once you have chosen to participate in this paradigm shift and
"suit up for the team," you will begin to see ways you can contribute

because your consciousness will be different. You will not only see what you can *start* doing, but you will realize things you are presently doing that you wish to stop, since they perpetuate the outmoded paradigm. I do have a few suggestions for you to consider—not a comprehensive list but somewhat universal for anyone engaging in this cultural transformation:

- Become emotionally mature; start therapy with a professional skilled in helping people distinguish emotions from moods or mental states so they can be identified as processes, rather than unconsciously harbored or stifled.
- Ruthlessly examine the underlying assumptions in the way you think.
- Engage others in dialogue; have meaningful conversations about what's really important to each of you.
- Stand tall for your values—in your actions, not just your words.
- Learn how to think more systemically; become a scholar of systems dynamics so you will recognize when systems are out of whack and where and how to intercede when they are.
- Become literate in unfamiliar disciplines, like physics, economics, biology or anthropology, so you can learn from several of them at the same time.
- Broaden your understanding of how all cultures and systems interact and influence one another.
- Learn to meditate, take time to relax, schedule time for retreat on a regular basis.
- End your addictions; identify the compulsions and obsessions you possess and stop them.

Before you can seriously entertain any of these suggestions, or embrace any changes to your personal lifestyle, please be reminded that you will need to confront one of the toughest adversaries known to human beings: the unwillingness to get uncomfortable, which in this case means to take on something that is unfamiliar. Actually, human beings may endure discomfort for decades, but only because it is *familiar* discomfort. And habits like these can be difficult to break, even ones we claim we want to stop. So, *be willing to be uncomfortable with the unfamiliar.*

The good news for conscious evolution is that not every human being has to be willing to change. Only a portion of us needs to be willing to start the change happening, to create what is popularly called "the tipping point" so that the shift in thinking and behavior begins and the tide is turned.

Toward the end of his bestselling book, *Confessions of an Economic Hit Man*, John Perkins also has some advice for what to do. His final two paragraphs include his personal suggestions. After baring his own soul in the previous pages and examining his own demons, Perkins recognizes his role and responsibility for contributing to a system he actually abhorred. He writes:

> For me, confessing was an essential part of my personal wake-up call. Like all confessions, it is the first step toward redemption. [*He then talks to the reader.*] Now it is your turn. You need to make your own confession. When you come clean on who you are, why you are here during this time in history, why you have done the things you have—the ones you are proud of, and those others—and where you intend to go next, you will experience an immediate sense of relief. It may be nothing less than euphoric.

Then Perkins suggests some questions to ask yourself.

> What do I need to confess? How have I deceived myself and others? Where have I deferred? Why

have I allowed myself to be sucked into a system that I know is unbalanced? What will I do to make sure our children, and all children everywhere, are able to fulfill the dream of our Founding Fathers, the dream of life, liberty, and the pursuit of happiness? What changes will I commit to making in my attitudes and perceptions?

This is the introspection we all need to make a regular part of our lives, like eating meals and exercising. Perkins continues:

> These are the essential questions of our time. Each of us needs to answer them in our own way and to express our answers clearly, unequivocally. Paine and Jefferson and all the other patriots are watching over our shoulders. Their words continue to inspire us today. The spirits of those men and women who left their farms and fishing boats and headed out to confront the mighty British Empire, and of those who fought to emancipate the slaves during the Civil War, and of those who sacrificed their lives to protect the world from fascism, speak to us.

He then brings us back to the present:

> The hour is ours. It is now time for each and every one of us to step up to the battle line, to ask the important questions, to search our souls for our own answers, and to take action . . . The coincidences of your life, and the choices you have made in response to them, have brought you to this point.[8]

CONSCIOUS LEADERSHIP

"Conscious leadership" is the term I coined in the early 1990s to describe a state of mind that includes heightened awareness of what is needed for the whole *and* taking responsible action based upon that awareness. As His Holiness the Dalai Lama has stated: "As people see their predicament clearly—that our fates are inextricably tied together, that life is a mutually interdependent web of relations—then universal responsibility becomes the only sane choice for thinking people."

Conscious leaders are the more mature stand-takers opposing many of the current trends and advocating new approaches. This may cause them to be branded "conservative" by the liberals or "leftist" by the Right Wing because they will not be wedded to a single ideology. Conscious leaders transcend left and right, conservative and liberal. They stand for a new way for us all to exist in a sustainable world *together*, focused on our commonalities, not exaggerating our differences and warring with one another verbally or militaristically.

Many of these people are already speaking out and, as is often done when a paradigm change is in its beginnings, they are being shouted down. Some are quite young, some older, many from outside the elite circle of power brokers. It takes sophisticated discernment to distinguish between the extremists who continue to drive a wedge between the warring ideologies and the radicals who are insisting on a way toward a future whereby all human beings continue to evolve and grow in a climate of dignity, respect and security.

Conscious leaders possess a unique combination of strengths—a powerful and informed vision for a sustainable species, as well as the spiritual chutzpah to act on their vision. In contrast to traditional leaders who spend years building resumes, acquiring wealth and power, playing politics to get the titles and rank, these new leaders know that the way to a better future is incredibly simple.

These leaders of conscious evolution already exist in government, business, education and most other segments of our society. But their populations are small, relatively low profile, and widely dispersed. They have evolved through personal introspection, usually some spiritual practice, and often all by themselves. They do not necessarily know of one another.

Conscious leaders exist in all levels of organizational systems. Some are independent and work as consultants. They are showing up in more situations, and in greater numbers, around the world. While they are still relatively silent, they are starting to make noise.

Here are a few comparisons between conscious leadership and traditional leadership:

Traditional Leadership	Conscious Leadership
Politics prevails	Truth-telling prevails
Tends to lead forcefully	Leads with presence
Tends to be dominating	Possesses dominion, mastery
Protects own image	Serves those who follow
Intimidates, rules, manipulates	Inspires, evokes greatness
Relies on form, structure	Trusts in Self, other
Outer-directed	Inner-directed
Eventually becomes incompetent	Continues to grow and learn
More adolescent, even if highly functional	Adult, wiser and more mature
Strong persona, maintains image	Authentic and genuine

As conscious leaders grow in numbers and take greater responsibility for the future, organizations remaining committed to the status quo will not only experience a "brain drain" of monumental proportions, they will also suffer a "consciousness drain" that could result in their eventual demise. We are starting to see the failure of these dinosaur organizations—be they banks, corporations, universities or governments—who refuse to transcend the old consciousness and embrace the new. After all, this is a milestone in the evolution of humankind, and those who are not aligned with and prepared for the emerging paradigm will become obsolete with the old one as it loses credibility and legitimacy.

Conscious leaders are coming from many unexpected quarters. They include disillusioned corporate executives, young people who don't know they aren't supposed to be able to do what hasn't been done before, and women who possess an innate perspective about community and sustainability. They will sometimes include someone who is part of the existing system but nevertheless sees the wisdom in changing our collective worldview to one that offers greater hope, inspires a larger vision, honors the human spirit, and sets the stage for humanity to fulfill a higher destiny. They will be stand-takers.

GLOBAL TRANSFORMATION: OPPORTUNITIES FOR NEW PIONEERS

Are we up for it? Are we game to stop adapting ourselves to our conditions and start adapting our conditions to fit us? We are capable of creating workplaces, businesses and schools that serve our humanity rather than forcing ourselves to conform to these industrialized systems created like nineteenth-century factories. We are capable of creating an entire world that is people friendly—made for humankind, not for robots or machines. We have the capacity to do this if we are clear, authentic and healthy representatives of the human race.

Many movements to make the world a better place are populated with people who are sacrificing themselves for the cause, playing the part of modern day martyrs. However, the Great Dream is not a call to martyrdom. It is an opportunity to serve, to play in a really meaningful game, to get involved in something that is timely (never could have been done before now), excitingly new (as in never been done before in human history), immensely creative (what could be more creative than a new world?) and incredibly challenging (you bet!). It is an opportunity to play with some great people, real visionaries who are also smart, global citizens who think outside the box, whose ideas transcend national boundaries.

This is an opportunity for pioneers who want to open a new frontier in human evolution. It is a chance to work toward something immensely meaningful; namely, shifting the whole context of human reality so all those charities that tug at our hearts—the starving children in Africa, sick people in remote regions of the world, victims of genocide, all efforts to alleviate suffering or heal a wound—will start transforming from their source.

We deserve the reality that we empower with our legitimacy. We deserve the reality we condone or put up with for whatever reason. We deserve the reality we get, for we are the ones allowing it to continue. Is this the reality we want? I recall the words of one of the sages from the human potential movement in the 1970s; it went something like, "We either have what we want or the reasons why we don't."

Duane Elgin writes:

> We are a visual species; we cannot consciously build a positive future that we have not first *collectively* imagined. When we can see a sustainable and promising future, we can build it. Actions can then come quickly and voluntarily. Voluntary or self-organized action will be vital to success, as hundreds of millions of people will be required to act in cooperation with one another. With local to global communication, we can mobilize ourselves purposefully, and each can contribute their unique talents to the creation of a life-affirming future.[9]

CONCLUSION

I'd like to repeat a cautionary note from dignitarian-culture advocate Bob Fuller. He writes:

> Of course, when set beside current events, this model of [a new] society . . . may very well sound utopian. Emerging social models always do until moments

before a new consensus displaces a prevailing one. As it turned out, Martin Luther King Jr's "I have a dream" speech was not a pipe dream. It was a timely prophecy of America's imminent emergence as a multicultural society, with global ramifications as well.[10]

And Perkins has another reminder for Americans:

We must shake ourselves awake. We who live in the most powerful nation history has ever known must stop worrying so much about the outcome of soap operas, football games, quarterly balance sheets, and the daily Dow Jones average, and must instead re-evaluate who we are and where we want our children to end up. The alternative to stopping to ask ourselves the important questions is simply too dangerous.[11]

Jacob Needleman writes about the desire to "rediscover the soul of America" and points to the ideal of self-improvement, which has its roots in all humankind but certainly was behind the founding of these United States. He points to it and writes that this is "an ideal that resonates to the great wisdom traditions of human history—[it] lies at the heart of early American individualism."[12]

There is a greater destiny awaiting us as a species—a destiny that we have scarcely come to know. The American Dream envisioned in 1776 might have been an early peek into this destiny, but it was focused on creating an all new society in the Americas. This was a huge step at that time—to forgo monarchy and start a brand new human experiment.

Now, a quarter of a millennium later, it is time to take another huge step, focused on creating an all new society *for the world*. It is time to be united, as Pierre Teilhard de Chardin foresaw, "in a common passion" or a unifying "sense of Earth." The Great Dream is focused on all of humankind. It is hardly about competing with one another over the symbols of a consumptive materialism.

As Einstein, Bertrand Russell, and their colleagues reminded us in 1955, "There lies before us, if we choose, continual progress in happiness, knowledge, and wisdom."[13] But we must choose it this time. It will not default to us if we allow things to go along the way they have been.

The question before us is whether we are to remain the slaves to our circumstances or achieve mastery over them. Italian psychologist Piero Ferrucci writes in *Inevitable Grace* that:

> . . . there exists in us a whole identity, endowed with qualities and abilities of the highest order, which we do not recognize we have. We therefore live a life far below our psychological and spiritual means. Also, there are ways of discovering—or rediscovering— who we are and of what we are capable.[14]

A world that works for everyone is possible. It appears to be the next big challenge for humanity—to achieve a world at peace, with everyone's basic needs being met, and freedom for everyone to pursue their dreams. If this isn't our next challenge as a species, then what is? What could possibly compete with this challenge for the next step in our growing up and accepting our destiny as mature human beings?

Spanish philosopher George Santayana addressed the limitations we place on ourselves most succinctly: "We must welcome the future, remembering that soon it will be the past; we must respect the past, remembering that once it was all that was humanly possible."

And Don Miguel Ruiz's writings and the Toltec Wisdom remind us:

> For thousands of years we have been searching for happiness. Happiness is the lost paradise. Humans

have worked so hard to reach this point, and this part of the evolution of the mind. This is the future of humanity. This way of life is possible, and it's in your hands. Moses called it the Promised Land. Jesus called it Heaven, and the Toltecs call it a New Dream.[15]

Here I'm calling it the Great Dream—that sacred evolution to a state of exalted consciousness that we have all longed for. We've had glimpses of it, certainly—some so faint that we weren't sure we saw what we saw. We might have even convinced ourselves that we never saw anything; that it must have been our imagination. And sure enough, it was! Our imagination does see the possibility, right here, close at hand. It feels so close sometimes!

And the best thing is that all we need to do is change our thinking and act accordingly. We simply have to remove the legitimacy we are presently giving to the old system and take a stand for "the new legitimacy." It is really that easy. Ferrucci's conclusion: "To deny such a possibility is to belie our humanity."

Let us exit our absurdities and reenter the path toward our destiny as a civilized and blessed society. Let us "take history by the throat" and create a future for all the world that is more befitting, civil and self-respecting for mature human beings. Let us not only "dare to know," as Kant challenged us more than two centuries ago, but let us also dare to dream the Great Dream and create a world that allows us all to live and work together with the freedom to pursue aliveness, greatness, success, and true happiness.

ENDNOTES

INTRODUCTION

1. Ian Morris, private e-mail exchange, April 15, 2011:

   Dear John, Thanks for your message. In my book (*Why the West Rules – For Now*) I design an index for measuring social development, which suggests that if development keeps rising across the 21st century at the same speed that it increased across the 20th century, the miracle of compound interest will mean that development will rise four (not five) times as much in the next 100 years as it's done in the previous 15,000. However, I also point out that in the past, periods of rapidly increasing social development have tended to generate forces that oppose and undermine development, with the result that we sometimes get great social collapses – which may be an equally plausible scenario for the 21st century.

   The exact phrasing I use in my book is: "In an interview in 2000, the economist Jeremy Rifkin suggested that 'Our way of life is likely to be more fundamentally transformed in the next several decades than in the previous 1,000 years.' That sounds extreme, but if Figure 12.1 really does show the shape of the future, Rifkin's projection is in fact a serious understatement. Between 2000 and 2050, according to the graph, social development will rise twice as much as in the previous fifteen thousand years; and by 2103 it will have doubled again." (p. 591). All best, Ian

2. Jerome C. Glenn and Theodore J. Gordon, "Executive Summary," *2004 State of the Future* (American Council for the United Nations University, 2004),

1,   *http://www.millennium-project.org/millennium/Executive-Summary-2004.pdf*

CHAPTER 1

1. Noah Feldman, *Divided by God: America's Church-State Problem – and What We Should Do About It* (New York: Farrar, Straus & Giroux, 2005), 10.
2. R. Buckminster Fuller, *Critical Path* (New York: St. Martin's Press, 1981), xxv.
3. Duane Elgin, *The Living Universe: Where Are We? Who Are We? Where Are We Going?* (San Francisco: Berrett-Koehler, 2009), 116.
4. Immanual Kant, "What Is Enlightenment?" 1784 essay republished in *An Answer to the Question* (New York: Penguin Books, 1991), 1.
5. Willis Harman, "Unemployment: Spiritual or Economic Crisis?" *The New Leaders* (March/April 1996): 1.
6. Michael Dowd, *Thank God for Evolution* (New York: Plume/Penguin Group, 2009), 128.
7. Barbara Marx Hubbard, *Conscious Evolution: Awakening the Power of Our Social Potential* (Novato, CA: New World Library, 1998), 24, *http://www.barbaramarxhubbard.com*
8. R. Buckminster Fuller, *Operating Manual for Spaceship Earth* (Baden, Switzerland: Lars Müller Publishers, 2008), 128. Available free online at *http://classes.dma.ucla.edu/Winter09/9-1/_pdf/3-fuller_operating-manual.pdf*
9. Paul R. Ehrlich and Anne H. Ehrlich, *The Dominant Animal: Human Evolution and the Environment* (Alameda, CA: Island Press, 2008), Epilogue.

CHAPTER 2

1. Nassim Taleb, *The Black Swan* (New York: Random House, 2007), 144.
2. Harlan Cleveland, *Nobody in Charge* (San Francisco: Jossey-Bass, 2002), 54.
3. Bernard Lietaer, *www.lietaer.com* (viewed March 10, 2009).
4. "Stop Cancer Before It Starts Campaign: How to Win the Losing War Against Cancer," report by The Cancer Prevention Coalition (2003).
5. Jerry Krueger and Emily Killham, "Why Dilbert Is Right," *Gallup Management Journal* (March 9, 2006), *http://gmj.gallup.com/content/21802/Why-Dilbert-Right.aspx*
6. Peter Senge, in an interview with Prasad Kaipa, *Three Circles: A Newsletter from The Kaipa Group* (January 2007), *http://kaipagroup.com/newsletter/January2007_newsletter.html*
7. Chris Thomson, "A Second Enlightenment," *Club of Amsterdam Journal* (August 2007), *http://www.clubofamsterdam.com/press.asp?contentid=706#article03*

8. Frank Furedi, "The market in fear," *Spiked-Online* (September 26, 2005), *http://www.spiked-online.com/Articles/0000000CAD7B.htm*.

9. Elgin, *Living Universe*, 115.

10. "A Course of Love," manuscript presented by M. Perron and D. Odegard in 2000, basis for a book of the same title published by New World Library, 2001.

11. Peter Kingsley, *Reality* (Pt. Reyes, CA: The Golden Sufi Center, 2003). *http://www.peterkingsley.org/pages.cfm?ID=6*.

12. David Batstone, "Right Reality: Are You Afraid?" *The Wag*, e-zine column (April 20, 2005).

13. Morris Berman, *Dark Ages America: The Final Phase of Empire* (New York: W.W. Norton, 2006), 245.

14. Tom Atlee, private e-mail (July 11, 2006).

15. James Hollis, personal e-mail (December 21, 2010).

CHAPTER 3

1. Howard Thurman, interview with Ronald Eyre prepared for *The Long Search*, BBC television series on world religions, *http://www.youtube.com/watch?v=B85dsSqBauw* (viewed April 4, 2011), published in *God and Human Freedom: A Festschrift in Honor of Howard Thurman*, Henry J. Young, ed. (Richmond, IN: Friends United Press, 1983). Eyre was a graduate of Oxford University and a writer of TV drama for the BBC.

2. Willigis Jaeger, *Mysticism for Modern Times* (Liquori, MO: Liquori/Triumph, 2006), xxiv.

3. Milton Friedman, "The Social Responsibility of Business Is to Increase Its Profits," *The New York Times Magazine* (September 13, 1970), accessed online February 24, 2008, *http://www.colorado.edu/studentgroups/libertarians/issues/friedman-soc-resp-business.html*

4. Jeff Gates, *Democracy at Risk: Rescuing Main Street from Wall Street: A Populist Vision for the 21st Century* (New York: Perseus Books, 2000), 17.

5. Eckhart Tolle, *The New Earth* (Dutton, 2005), 22, *http://www.eckhart-tolle.com/*

6. Jaeger, *Mysticism*, Introduction.

7. "A Course of Love," 103.

8. Amartya Sen, *Identity and Violence: The Illusion of Destiny* (New York: W.W. Norton, 2006), 1.

9. Tolle, *New Earth*, 77.

10. Ibid.

11. Robert W. Fuller, *All Rise: Somebodies, Nobodies, and the Politics of Dignity* (San Francisco: Berrett-Koehler, 2006), 17, *http://breakingranks.net/*

12. Ibid.

13. Tolle, *New Earth*, 77.
14. "Tale of Two Dogs," by Native American tribal leader quoted in Rolf Gates, *Meditations from the Mat* (Anchor Books, 2002), 360.
15. Alan Seale, *Create a World That Works: Tools for Personal and Global Transformation* (Newburyport, MA: Weiser Books, 2011), 47.

CHAPTER 4

1. "Holbrooke on Iraq, Mandela, and the Quest for World Peace," *Leaders* magazine, (July-September, 2004).
2. Vaclav Havel, Stanford University, Lecture 29, September 1994.
3. R. Buckminster Fuller, *Operating Manual*, 31 (see chap. 1, n. 8).

CHAPTER 5

1. Alex Scott, "The Implications of Fatalism," Internet essay, *http://www.angelfire.com/md2/timewarp/fatalism.html*
2. "Some Startling Statistics," Robyn Jackson, *HumorWriters.org*, Stats source: ParaPublishing, Dan Poynter (*http://www.humorwriters.org/startlingstats.html*)
3. Doreen Carvajal, "Mass-Media Use by Consumers, 1996,"*The New York Times (August 24, 1997).*
4. National Literacy Trust (UK), "Forty Percent of Britons Never Read Books!" *The Telegraph* (27 May 2002).
5. Peter M. Senge, *The Fifth Discipline: The Art & Practice of the Learning Organization*, (Doubleday/Currency, 1990), 69.
6. FDIC, "The Effect of Consumer Interest Rate Deregulation on Credit Card Volumes, Charge-Offs, and the Personal Bankruptcy Rate," *Bank Trends* report #98-05 (March, 1998).
7. "Beyond Greed and Scarcity," interview with Bernard Lietaer by Sarah Van Gelder, editor of *YES! The Journal of Positive Futures* (viewed April 28, 2011), *http://www.transaction.net/press/interviews/lietaer0497.html*
8. "Open Debate," a conversation between John Seeley Brown and Shannon O'Brien, *Fast Company* (March 2006), 144.
9. "Another Sign of the Digital Age," *Discovery* magazine, August 2005. "Does email make you dumber," by Anne Casselman, *Discover Magazine*, August 2005 issue, published online August 6, 2005 (*http://discovermagazine.com/2005/aug/email-make-you-dumber*)
10. Andrew Bard Schmookler, *The Illusion of Choice: How the Market Economy Shapes Our Destiny* (State University of New York Press, 1993).
11. Jeff Goodell,"The Prophet of Climate Change: James Lovelock,"*RollingStone.com* (posted November 1, 2007), *http://www.rollingstone.com/politics/blogs/national-affairs/the-prophet-of-climate-change-james-lovelock-20071019*

12. Jeff Gates, "Globalization's Challenge: Attuning the Global to the Local," *Reflections*, Society for Organizational Learning, MIT (Summer 2002).
13. "Homes have more TVs than people," Associated Press, reported on CNN September 22, 2006.
14. "Rich still getting wealthier," *USA Today* (December 6, 2006).
15. Vaclav Havel, Stanford University, Lecture 29, September 1994.
16. Jeff Gates, *Democracy at Risk: Rescuing Main Street from Wall Street: A Populist Vision for the 21st Century* (Perseus Books, 2000).
17. Ibid, also see endnote 12.
18. Joel E. Cohen, "Human Population Grows Up," *Scientific American* (September 2005), *http://www.scientificamerican.com/article.cfm?id=human-population-grows-up*
19. Elgin, *Living Universe*.

CHAPTER 6

1. "A More Secure World: Our Shared Responsibility," Report of the Secretary-General's High-level Panel on Threats, Challenges and Change, United Nations (2004), *http://www.un.org/secureworld/report.pdf*
2. Patricia Aburdene, *Megatrends 2010: The Rise of Conscious Capitalism* (Hampton Roads Publishing, 2007), 5.
3. Eugene Taylor, *Shadow Culture: Psychology and Spirituality in America* (Counterpoint Press, 2000), 6.
4. Alcoholics Anonymous, *Twelve Steps and Twelve Traditions* (New York: The A.A. Grapevine, Inc. and Alcoholics Anonymous World Services, Inc., 2003).
5. Peter Russell, *The Global Brain: Speculations on the Evolutionary Leap to Planetary Consciousness* (J.P. Tarcher, 1983).
6. David Kyle, "Systemic Causality and the Nature of Organizations," paper presented at Eight Annual Standing Conference on Educational Research, Yale University (May 2005), 5.
7. Peter Drucker, *Post-Capitalist Society* (Harper Collins, 1993), 142-43.
8. Bernard Lietaer, *The Future of Money: Creating New Wealth, Work and a Wiser World* (Random House Pty London, 2001), (*http://www.lietaer.com/*)
9. Ibid., 324-325.

CHAPTER 7

1. Paul H. Ray and Sherry Ruth Anderson, *The Cultural Creatives: How 50 Million People Are Changing the World* (Three Rivers Press, 2001).
2. Patricia Cranton and Laurence Robert Cohen, "Spirals of Learning," *National Teaching & Learning Forum* 9:5 (2000).

3. "The 2007 Shift Report: Evidence of a World Transforming," Institute of Noetic Sciences (March 2007), 38, 41, *http://www.shiftreport.org/ShiftReport2007.htm*

4. Kingsley, *Reality*, 468 (see chap. 2, n. 11).

5. James Surowiecki, *The Wisdom of Crowds: Why the Many Are Smarter Than the Few and How Collective Wisdom Shapes Business, Economies, Societies and Nations* (Doubleday, 2004), 107.

6. Mark Gerzon, *Leading Through Conflict: How Successful Leaders Transform Differences into Opportunities* (Harvard Business School Press, 2006), *http://www.amazon.com/Leading-Through-Conflict-Differences-Opportunities/dp/159139919X/ref=sr_1_1?ie=UTF8&s=books&qid=1207332858&sr=1-1*

7. "Europeans united in diversity," *http://europa.eu/abc/european_countries/languages/english/index_en.htm* (viewed April 28, 2011).

8. Gerzon, *Leading Through Conflict.*

9. Riane Eisler, *The Chalice and the Blade: Our History, Our Future* (HarperSanFrancisco, 1987), 186, *http://www.partnershipway.org/about-cps*

CHAPTER 8

1. Willis Harman, *Global Mind Change: The Promise of the 21ˢᵗ Century* (San Francisco: Berrett-Koehler, 1998), vii, *http://www.bkconnection.com/ProdDetails.asp?ID=1576750299&PG=1&Type=AUTH&PCS=BKP*

2. Jaeger, *Mysticism*, 134 (see chap. 3, n. 2).

3. John Renesch, *Getting to the Better Future: A Matter of Conscious Choosing* (New Business Books, 2000), 49-50, *http://www.GettingToTheBetterFuture.com*

4. "Yogi on Wall Street: The Practical Value of Values in Business," an unpublished manuscript by Paul Mlotok, private e-mail based on Mlotok's manuscript, August 13, 2004.

5. Paul Dolan, *True to Our Roots: Fermenting a Business Revolution* (Bloomberg Press, 2003), 161, *http://www.pauldolanspeaking.com/site/index.php?option=com_content&task=view&id=15&Itemid=29*

6. Walter Truett Anderson, *Reality Isn't What It Used To Be* (Harper Collins, 1990), 73-74, *http://www.waltanderson.info/work6.htm*

7. Ibid.

8. Ibid.

9. Kyle, "Systemic Causality," 5 (see chap. 6, n. 6).

10. Ibid.

11. "A Course of Love," xxx (see chap. 2, n. 10).

12. Adam Kahane, *Solving Tough Problems: An Open Way of Talking, Listening and Creating New Realities* (San Francisco: Berrett-Koehler, 2004). *http://www.bkconnection.com/ProdDetails.asp?ID=9781576754641&PG=1&Type=AUTH&PCS=BKP*

CHAPTER 9

1. Kingsley, *Reality*, 340.
2. Ibid., 340-341.
3. Michael Dowd, *Thank God for Evolution* (New York: Plume/Penguin Group, 2009), 128.
4. "Whole-System Integration," a paper presented by Mel Toomey, Center for Leadership Studies, MAOL class, Sanderling Resort, June 2005. Toomey teaches the *Master of Arts in Organizational Leadership* (MAOL) course, accredited by The Graduate Institute.
5. Kazuo Inamori, *A Compass to Fulfillment: Passion and Spirituality in Life and Business* (McGraw-Hill, 2010), 98-99.
6. Raj Sisodia, Jag Smith and David B. Wolfe, *Firms of Endearment: How World-Class Companies Profit from Passion and Purpose* (Wharton School Publishing, 2007), 193.
7. Bernard Lietaer, *www.lietaer.com* (viewed March 10, 2009).
8. John Perkins, *Confessions of an Economic Hit Man* (San Francisco: Berrett-Koehler, 2004), 224-225, *http://www.bkconnection.com/ProdDetails.asp?ID=1576753018&PG=1&Type=BL&PCS=BKP*
9. Elgin, *The Living Universe*, 134.
10. Robert W. Fuller, *All Rise*, 123 (see chap. 3, n. 11).
11. Perkins, *Confessions*, 225.
12. Jacob Needleman, *The American Soul* (Jeremy P. Tarcher/Putnam, 2003), 39.
13. "Bertrand Russell & Albert Einstein: Manifesto," signed by Bertrand Russell, Albert Einstein, Linus Pauling and others, London, 9 July 1955, *http://en.wikisource.org/wiki/Russell-Einstein_Manifesto*
14. Piero Ferrucci, *Inevitable Grace: Guides to Your Self-Realization* (Jeremy P. Tarcher, 1990), 348.
15. Don Miguel Ruiz, *The Four Agreements: A Toltec Wisdom Book* (Amber-Allen Publishing, 1997), 138.

BIBLIOGRAPHY

Alcoholics Anonymous. *Twelve Steps and Twelve Traditions*. New York: The A.A. Grapevine and Alcoholics Anonymous World Services, 2003.

Anderson, Walter Truett. *The Next Enlightenment*. St. Martin's Press, 2003. *http://www.waltanderson.info/work1.htm*

_____. *Reality Isn't What It Used To Be*. Harper Collins, 1990. *http://www.waltanderson.info/work6.htm*

"Another Sign of the Digital Age," *Discovery* (August 2005).

Associated Press. "Rich still getting wealthier," *USA Today* (December 6, 2006).

Atlee, Tom. Private e-mail (July 11, 2006).

"Average CEO Salary Soars Again, by 38% to $15.2 Million," *Currents in Commerce* 21, no. 5 (July 17, 2007).

Batstone, David. "Right Reality: Are You Afraid?" *The Wag* (April 20, 2005). Online newsletter for *Worthwhile* magazine.

Berman, Morris. *Dark Ages America: The Final Phase of Empire*. W.W. Norton, 2006.

"Bertrand Russell & Albert Einstein: Manifesto," signed by Bertrand Russell, Albert Einstein, Linus Pauling and others (London, 9 July 1955). *http://en.wikisource.org/wiki/Russell-Einstein_Manifesto*

"Beyond Greed and Scarcity: An interview with Bernard Lietaer" by Sarah van Gelder in *YES! A Journal of Positive Futures* (Spring 1997). *http://www.yesmagazine.org/article.asp?ID=886*

"Book illustrates the fundamentals of fundamentalism." Book review by Curtis Hart, *Science & Theology News* (October 19, 2005).

Bronson, Po. E-mail about his new book, *Why Do I Love These People: Honest and Amazing Stories of Real Families* (November 15, 2005).

Buber, Martin. *I and Thou.* Translation by Ronald Gregor Smith. Macmillan, 1958.

Carvajal, Doreen. "Mass-Media Use by Consumers, 1996," *The New York Times (August 24, 1997).*

"Charlie Rose Show" interview with Kim Clark, Dean, Harvard Business School, PBS Television (July 31, 2005). Watch video at *http://www.charlierose.com/view/interview/801*

Cleveland, Harlan. *Nobody in Charge.* Jossey-Bass, 2002.

Cohen, Joel E. "Human Population Grows Up," *Scientific American* (September 2005).

"A Course of Love." Manuscript presented by M. Perron and D. Odegard in 2000, basis for a book of the same time title published by New World Library, 2001.

Cranton, Patricia and Laurence Robert Cohen. "Spirals of Learning," *National Teaching and Learning Forum* 9, no. 5 (2000).

Dolan, Paul. *True to Our Roots: Fermenting a Business Revolution.* Bloomberg Press, 2003. *http://www.pauldolanspeaking.com/site/index.php?option=com_content&task=view&id=15&Itemid=29*

Dowd, Michael. *Thank God for Evolution.* New York: Plume/Penguin Group, 2009.

Drucker, Peter. *Post-Capitalist Society.* Harper Collins, 1993.

"Drug Use Trends," The White House Office of National Drug Control Policy (ONDCP) Information Clearinghouse (October 2002).

Ehrlich, Paul R. and Anne H. Ehrlich. *The Dominant Animal: Human Evolution and the Environment.* Island Press, 2008.

Eisler, Riane. *The Chalice and the Blade: Our History, Our Future.* HarperSanFrancisco, 1987. *http://www.partnershipway.org/learn-more/partnership-books/the-chalice-and-the-blade*

Elgin, Duane. *The Living Universe: Where Are We? Who Are We? Where Are We Going?* San Francisco: Berrett-Koehler, 2009.

"Examining the Real Agenda of the Religious Far Right," Karen Armstrong panelist, Open Center and SUNY Graduate Center, April 29-30, 2005 (aired on C-Span TV).

FDIC. "The Effect of Consumer Interest Rate Deregulation on Credit Card Volumes, Charge-Offs, and the Personal Bankruptcy Rate," *Bank Trends* report #98-05 (March, 1998).

Feldman, Noah. *Divided by God: America's Church-State Problem – and What We Should Do About It.* New York: Farrar, Straus & Giroux, 2005.

Ferrucci, Piero. *Inevitable Grace: Guides to Your Self-Realization.* Jeremy P. Tarcher, 1990.

Frank, Robert. "U.S. Led a Resurgence Last Year Among Millionaires World-Wide," *Wall Street Journal* (June 15, 2004).

Friedman, Milton. *Capitalism and Freedom.* Chicago: University of Chicago Press, 1962.

_____. "The Social Responsibility of Business Is to Increase Its Profits," *The New York Times Magazine* (September 13, 1970), accessed February 24, 2008. *http://www.colorado.edu/studentgroups/libertarians/issues/friedman-soc-resp-business.html*

"From Gutenberg to Gates (and beyond...): Education for an Online World," compiled and presented by Ian Jukes, keynote address, InfoSavvy Group, TechEd 2001 Convention, Ontario, California. *http://www.usdla.org/html/journal/MAY01_Issue/article01.html*

Fuller, R. Buckminster. *Critical Path.* St. Martin's Press, 1981.

_____. *Operating Manual for Spaceship Earth.* Buckminster Fuller Institute, available free online at *http://classes.dma.ucla.edu/Winter09/9-1/_pdf/3-fuller_operating-manual.pdf*

Fuller, Robert W. *All Rise: Somebodies, Nobodies, and the Politics of Dignity.* San Francisco: Berrett-Koehler, 2006. *http://breakingranks.net/*

_____. *Somebodies and Nobodies: Overcoming the Abuse of Rank.* New Society Publishers, 2003. *http://www.breakingranks.net/weblog/somebodies-and-nobodies*

Furedi, Frank. "The market in fear," *Spiked-Online* (September 26, 2005). *http://www.spiked-online.com/Articles/0000000CAD7B.htm*

Gates, Jeff. *Democracy at Risk: Rescuing Main Street from Wall Street: A Populist Vision for the 21st Century.* Perseus Books, 2000.

_____. "Globalization's Challenge: Attuning the Global to the Local," *Reflections* (Summer 2002). Society for Organizational Learning, MIT.

Gerzon, Mark. *Leading Through Conflict: How Successful Leaders Transform Differences into Opportunities.* Harvard Business School Press, 2006. *http://www.amazon.com/Leading-Through-Conflict-Differences-Opportunities/dp/159139919X/ref=sr_1_1?ie=UTF8&s =books&qid=1207332858&sr=1-1*

Glenn, Jerome C. and Theodore J. Gordon. "Executive Summary," *2004 State of the Future.* American Council for the United Nations University, 2004. *http://www.millennium-project.org/millennium/ Executive-Summary-2004.pdf*

Global survey of knowledge workers conducted by Career Innovation Company, *The Wag,* David Batstone newsletter, April 13, 2006.

Godin, Seth. "The Threat of Pigeons and Other Fundamentalists," *Fast Company* (June 2003). *http://www.fastcompany.com/magazine/72/ sgodin.html*

Goodell, Jeff. "The Prophet of Climate Change: James Lovelock," *RollingStone.com* (posted November 1, 2007). *http://www.rollingstone.com/politics/blogs/national-affairs/ the-prophet-of-climate-change-james-lovelock-20071019*

Gopnik, Adam. "Jesus Laughed," book review, *The New Yorker* (April 17, 2006).

Gottleib, Elaine. "The Science of Addiction," adapted from "Just the Facts," published by the U.S. Substance Abuse and Mental Health Services Administration. EBSCO Publishing, 2006. *http://www. beliefnet.com/healthandhealing/getcontent.aspx?cid=14185&WT. mc_id=NL*

Harman, Willis. *Global Mind Change: The Promise of the 21st Century.* San Francisco: Berrett-Koehler, 1998. *http://www.bkconnection. com/ProdDetails.asp?ID=1576750299&PG=1&Type=AUTH&PCS =BKP*

_____. "Unemployment: Spiritual or Economic Crisis?" *The New Leaders* (March/April 1996).

"Holbrooke on Iraq, Mandela, and the Quest for World Peace," *Leaders* magazine (July-September, 2004).

Hollis, James. Personal e-mail dated December, 21, 2010.

"Homes have more TVs than people," reported on CNN September 22, 2006.

Hubbard, Barbara Marx. *Conscious Evolution: Awakening the Power of Our Social Potential.* New World Library, 1998. *http://www.barbaramarxhubbard.com*

Inamori, Kazuo. *A Compass to Fulfillment: Passion and Spirituality in Life and Business.* McGraw-Hill, 2010.

Institute of Noetic Sciences. *The 2007 Shift Report: Evidence of a World Transforming.* March 2007. *http://www.shiftreport.org/ShiftReport2007.htm*

"An Interview with Linus Torvalds," *First Monday* 3, no. 1 (March 2, 1998).

Jaeger, Willigis. *Mysticism for Modern Times.* Liquori, MO: Liquori/Triumph, 2006.

Johnston, Charles. "Creating the Story of Tomorrow," *Shift: At the Frontiers of Consciousness,* The Institute of Noetic Sciences (March-May 2005).

Joy, Bill. "Why the future doesn't need us," *Wired* magazine (April 2000).

Kahane, Adam. "Destino Colombia: A Scenario-Planning Process for the New Millennium," *Deeper News,* Global Business Network (1998). *http://www.gbn.com/consulting/article_details.php?id=34*

_____. "How to Change the World: Lessons for Entrepreneurs from Activists," speech delivered to *Fast Company*'s Real Time Conference, May 2000.

_____. "Preface: Notes on the Destino Colombia Process," *Deeper News* 9, no. 1, Global Business Network.

_____. *Solving Tough Problems: An Open Way of Talking, Listening and Creating New Realities.* San Francisco: Berrett-Koehler, 2004. *http://www.bkconnection.com/ProdDetails.asp?ID=9781576754641&PG=1&Type=AUTH&PCS=BKP*

Kamp, Jurriaan. "When doctors strike, fewer people die," *Ode* magazine, *http://www.the-boondocks.org/forum/index.php?t=msg&goto=36199&*

Kant, Immanuel. "What Is Enlightenment?" 1784 essay.

Kingsley, Peter. *Reality.* Pt. Reyes, CA: The Golden Sufi Center, 2003. *http://www.peterkingsley.org/pages.cfm?ID=6*

Krueger, Jerry and Emily Killham. "Why Dilbert Is Right," *Gallup Management Journal* (March 9, 2006).

Kyle, David. "Systemic Causality and the Nature of Organizations," paper presented at Eight Annual Standing Conference on Educational Research, Yale University, May 2005.

Lietaer, Bernard. *The Future of Money: Creating New Wealth, Work and a Wiser World.* Random House Pty London, 2001. *http://www.lietaer.com/writings/books/*

_____. *Of Human Wealth: New Currencies for a New World.* Citerra Press, 2008.

_____. *www.lietaer.com* (viewed March 10, 2009).

Mlotok, Paul. Private e-mail of August 13, 2004, based on his unpublished manuscript, "A More Secure World: Our Shared Responsibility," Report of the Secretary-General's High-level Panel on Threats, Challenges and Change. United Nations, 2004.

_____. "A Yogi on Wall Street: The Practical Use of Values in Business." Unpublished manuscript.

Musser, George. "The Climax of Humanity," *Scientific American* (September 2005).

National Literacy Trust (UK). "Forty Percent of Britons Never Read Books!" *The Telegraph (*27 May 2002).

National Literacy Trust (UK). "Half of U.S. Shuns Literature," *Guardian* (July 9, 2004).

Needleman, Jacob. *The American Soul.* Jeremy P. Tarcher/Putnam, 2003.

Nicholson, Peter J. "Harnessing the Wisdom of Crowds," remarks to The Fields Institute in Mathematical Sciences, Annual General Meeting, Toronto, June 15, 2006.

O'Neil, John. *The Paradox of Success: When Winning at Work Means Losing at Life.* Jeremy P. Tarcher/Putnam, 1994.

"Open Debate," a conversation between John Seeley Brown and Shannon O'Brien, *Fast Company* (March 2006): 144.

Paine, Thomas. *Common Sense.* 1776. Now available in paperback from Dover Publications, 1997.

Perkins, John. *Confessions of an Economic Hit Man.* San Francisco: Berrett-Koehler, 2004. *http://www.bkconnection.com/ProdDetails.asp?ID=1576753018&PG=1&Type=BL&PCS=BKP*

_____. "Hostages in the Amazon," *Dream Change Magazine* (Summer-Fall 2003):7.

Ray, Paul H. and Sherry Ruth Anderson. *The Cultural Creatives: How 50 Million People Are Changing the World.* Three Rivers Press, 2001.

Renesch, John. *Getting to the Better Future: A Matter of Conscious Choosing.* New Business Books, 2000. *http://www.GettingToTheBetterFuture.com*

_____. *"Memories of a Visionary Businessman,"* mini-keynote, February 2011. *http://www.renesch.com/newsletters/aha152.htm*

Ruiz, Don Miguel. *The Four Agreements: A Toltec Wisdom Book.* Amber-Allen Publishing, 1997.

Russell, Peter. *The Global Brain: Speculations on the Evolutionary Leap to Planetary Consciousness.* J.P. Tarcher, 1983.

Satin, Mark. "From material want to happiness, purpose and meaning," *Radical Middle* newsletter (March 15, 2006). *http://www.radicalmiddle.com/x_easterbrook.htm*

Schmookler, Andrew Bard. *The Illusion of Choice: How the Market Economy Shapes Our Destiny.* State University of New York Press, 1993.

Scott, Alex. "The Implications of Fatalism," an Internet essay. *http://www.angelfire.com/md2/timewarp/fatalism.html*

Seale, Alan. *Create a World That Works: Tools for Personal and Global Transformation.* Weiser Books, 2011.

Sen, Amartya. "Development as Freedom," *Personal Excellence* newsletter, Executive Excellence Publishing. *www.eep.com*

_____. *Identity and Violence: The Illusion of Destiny.* New York: W.W. Norton, 2006.

Senge, Peter. *The Fifth Discipline: The Art and Practice of the Learning Organization.* Doubleday/Currency, 1990.

_____. An interview with Prasad Kaipa, *Three Circles* newsletter #1, The Kaipa Group (January 2007). *http://kaipagroup.com/newsletter/January2007_newsletter.html*

Senge, Peter, C. Otto Scharmer, Joseph Jaworski, and Betty Sue Flowers. *Presence: Human Purpose and the Field of the Future. SOL, 2004.*

Smith, Adam. *The Wealth of Nations,* 1776. Now available in paperback from Prometheus Books, 1991.

Soros, George. *The Crisis of Global Capitalism*. Public Affairs, 1998.

"Spend More, Get Less," comparison matrix based on World Health Organization statistics, *Prevention* magazine (September 2005).

"Spendthrift Nation," *FRBSF Economic Letter no. 2005-30* (November 10, 2005). *http://www.frbsf.org/publications/economics/letter/2005/el2005-30.pdf*

Stewart, John. *Evolution's Arrow: The Direction of Evolution and the Future of Humanity*. Chapman Press, 2000.

"Stop Cancer Before It Starts Campaign: How to Win the Losing War Against Cancer," a report from The Cancer Prevention Coalition, 2003.

Surowiecki, James. *The Wisdom of Crowds: Why the Many Are Smarter Than the Few and How Collective Wisdom Shapes Business, Economies, Societies and Nations*. Doubleday, 2004.

"Tale of Two Dogs," from Native American tribal leader quoted in Rolf Gates, *Meditations from the Mat*. Anchor Books, 2002.

Taleb, Nassim. *The Black Swan*. Random House, 2007.

"Talking Point: Psychedelic Healing," an interview with Torsten Passie, *New Scientist* (April 15-21, 2006).

Taylor, Eugene. *Shadow Culture: Psychology and Spirituality in America*. Counterpoint Press, 2000.

Thomson, Chris. "A Second Enlightenment," *Club of Amsterdam Journal* (August 2007). *http://www.clubofamsterdam.com/press.asp?contentid=706#article03*

Thompson, Judith and James O'Dea. "Social Healing for a Fractured World," *Shift* (June-August, 2005). Institute of Noetic Sciences.

Thurman, Howard. From an interview with Ronald Eyre prepared for the BBC television series on world religions, *The Long Search*. Eyre was a graduate of Oxford University and a writer of TV drama for the BBC. Published in *God and Human Freedom: A Festschrift in Honor of Howard Thurman*, edited by Henry J. Young, Friends United Press, 1983.

Tolle, Eckhart. *The New Earth*. Dutton, 2005. *http://www.eckharttolle.com/*

Toomey, Mel. "Whole-System Integration," paper presented at Center for Leadership Studies, MAOL class, Sanderling Resort, June 2005.

Tutu, Archbishop Desmond. "Foreword by Chairperson," *Truth & Reconciliation Report.* South African Truth Commission, 1998.

Wallis, Claudia. "The New Science of Happiness," *Time* (January 17, 2005).

Yunus, Muhammad. *Banker to the Poor.* Public Affairs Books, 2003.

INDEX

Morris, Ian, xvii, 179
mortgage crisis. *See under* crisis
Mother Teresa, 143
mystics/mysticism, 2, 7, 20, 58,
    122, 153. *See also* philoso-
    phers/philosophy
myths, 3, 43
    debunking, 25-31
    market (*see* market myths)

N

Naisbitt, John, 126
Naked Ape (Morris), 18
National Endowment for the Arts
    (NEA), 78
National Institute on Drug Abuse,
    64
nation-state (vs. corporation), 87-
    88, 115
Natural Step, The, 98
nature/natural world, 17, 19, 26,
    27, 51
    dominating, 141, 166
    negative impact on, 32, 38, 48
    separation from, 90
    See also environment, natural
Needleman, Jacob, 11, 276
New America Foundation, 6
New York Times, The, 77-78, 90
Newman, Cardinal, 53
news/news media, 26, 57, 82, 105,
    114
Next American Spirituality, The
    (Gallup), 107
Next Enlightenment, The (Ander-
    son), 14
neuromarketing, 54. *See also* mar-
    ket; marketing
Nobel Peace Prize, 54, 117
nuclear weapons, 85, 132

O

Obama, Barak, 135
objectification (of people), 79-80
OD (organization development),
    130
Of Human Wealth (Lietaer), 85
offset printing, 105
Ohmae, Kenichi, 88
oil dependence (in the West), 63,
    131
"opinionism," 82-83, 133. *See also*
    mind
optimism, xix-xx
Ortega y Gasset, Jose, 46

P

Paine, Thomas, 4, 9, 45
paradigm changes/shifts, 147-148,
    149-156, 162, 168-169
    diagram: *Ending of One Para-
    digm/Birthing of New One*, 151
    diagram: *Paradigm Shift or
    Change of Context*, 72
paradox, 27, 51, 123, 155, 162
    particle/wave, 122
Parmenides, 123
"partnership model," 127
pay gap, 94-98. *See also* wealth
peak experience, 1, 153
Perkins, John, 170, 176
pessimism, xix-xx
Philips, "Fritz," 108
philosophers/philosophy, xix, 2, 7,
    11, 20, 122, 153
    Buddhist/Zen, 104-105, 133
    business, 87, 132
    democratic, 7, 11, 132
    of money, 116
    See also Buber, Martin; Emped-
    ocles; Gebster, Jean; Kant,
    Immanuel; Kuhn, Thomas;

Other Titles of Interest from Hohm Press/Kalindi Press

THE REVOLUTION FROM WITHIN
by J. Krishnamurti

Eastern and General Philosophy / Religious Studies
ISBN: 978-1-935387-05-3
320 pages + DVD insert; paperback; 5 ½ x 8 ½ inches; $19.95

"There must be a revolution in our thinking," declares the author, J. Krishnamurti (1895-1986), who remains one of the greatest philosophers and teachers of modern times. In this series of lectures, given in the U.S. and various cities throughout the world in the 1950s, he again confronts the habitual, projection-making mind, which fails to see *what is* while it absorbs itself in belief and illusion. Topics covered in these essays include: the process of change at all levels; the development of discipline; quieting the mind; self-awareness; and freedom from slavery to mind.

• • •

AS ONE IS
To Free the Mind from All Conditioning
by J. Krishnamurti

Eastern and General Philosophy / Religious Studies
ISBN: 978-1-890772-62-8
120 pages; paperback; 5 ½ x 8 ½ inches; $14.95

J. Krishnamurti remains one of the world's greatest philosophers and teachers. He deeply understands the operation of the human mind—particularly how our thinking lies at the root of all violence and suffering. In this series of previously unpublished lectures, he discusses a world in which booming productivity and scientific advancement *should* promise a happy future, but don't. He asks his listeners to consider that we are merely substituting comfortable myths for our fears, and living as if these myths were true.

This book patiently explains how to examine our assumptions; how to question our "conditioned" beliefs, and ultimately how to listen for truth…both within and from the world around us.

Visit our websites at www.hohmpress.com and www.kalindipress.com

Other Titles of Interest from Hohm Press/Kalindi Press

SELF OBSERVATION: THE AWAKENING OF CONSCIENCE
An Owner's Manual
by Red Hawk

Body, Mind & Spirit
ISBN: 978-1-890772-92-5
160 pages; paperback; 5 ½ x 8 ½ inches; $14.95

An in-depth examination of the much needed process of "self"-study known as self observation. Only when we "Know Thyself" through self observation practice, says the author, are we capable of being present to life with genuine conscience. The methods presented here are capable of restoring an individual's ability to pay attention, refining this into a fully functional and powerful tool for success in life and relationships. No other book on the market examines this practice in such detail. There are hundreds of books on self-help and meditation, but almost none on self-study via self-observation, and none with the depth of analysis, wealth of explication, and richness of experience which this book offers.

• • •

WOMEN HEALING WOMEN
A Model of Hope for Oppressed Women Everywhere
by William Keepin, Ph.D. and Cynthia Brix, M.Div.

Women's Studies / Social Issues
ISBN: 978-1-890772-88-8 (a Kalindi Press title)
320 pages; paperback; 6 x 9 inches; $19.95

Recounts the true story of MAHER, a remarkable center for battered women and children located near Pune, India. Since 1997, the project has provided refuge to more than 1250 women, many who might otherwise have been murdered, committed suicide, or starved to death. Maher is an interfaith community that honors all religions and strongly repudiates caste distinctions. Lends new hope for some of the gravest problems in India and around the world.

Visit our websites at www.hohmpress.com and www.kalindipress.com

Other Titles of Interest from Hohm Press/Kalindi Press

DIVINE DUALITY
The Power of Reconciliation between Women and Men
by William Keepin, Ph.D., with Cynthia Brix, M.Div. and Molly Dwyer, Ph.D.

Relationships / Gender Reconciliation
ISBN: 978-1-890772-74-1 (a Kalindi Press title)
320 pages; Paper; 6 x 9 inches; $16.95

This book demonstrates a revolutionary type of healing work between men and women, known as "gender reconciliation." Based on 15+ years of development, this process has created remarkable results within groups as diverse as nuns and priests in the Catholic Church, and most recently with members of the South African Parliament. The creative and compassionate methods designed by the author and his team at the Satyana Institute (of Freeland, Washington) take a broad leap beyond other approaches that are more oriented to addressing the needs of the couple. No other book currently deals with this subject with the depth of insight and proven results presented here.

• • •

FEAST OR FAMINE
Teachings on Mind and Emotions
by Lee Lozowick

Religious Studies
ISBN: 978-1-890772-79-6
256 pages; paperback; 6 x 9 inches; $19.95

This book focuses on core issues related to human suffering: *the mind* that doesn't "Know Thyself," and *the emotions* that create terrifying imbalance and unhappiness. The author, a spiritual teacher for over 35 years, details the workings of mind and emotions, offering practical interventions for when the mind or emotions are raging out of control. A practical handbook for meditators and anyone dedicated to "work on self."

Visit our websites at www.hohmpress.com and www.kalindipress.com

Other Titles of Interest from Hohm Press/Kalindi Press

YOGA MORALITY
Ancient Teachings in a Time of Global Crisis
by Georg Feuerstein

Yoga / Philosophy
ISBN: 978-1-890772-66-6
320 pages; Paper; 6 x 9 inches; $19.95

The spiritual and moral teachings of Yoga can serve as a life raft for those who want to live with integrity and without fear as humanity heads into turbulent waters. The book is a hard-hitting critique of the media hype surrounding Yoga, and an exploration of Yogic philosophy and practice to discover what it means to be a mature, moral person. It addresses the question: How are we to live consciously, responsibly, authentically, and without fear in the midst of mounting turmoil?

"Georg Feuerstein is not only vastly knowledgeable about the history and literature of spirituality, he is also a genuinely wise human being." — Richard Heinberg, core faculty, New College of California, and author *The Party's Over: Oil, War and the Fate of Industrial Societies*

• • •

THE JUMP INTO LIFE: *Moving Beyond Fear*
by Arnaud Desjardins
Foreword by Richard Moss, M.D.

Self-Help / Spirituality
ISBN: 0-934252-42-4
278 pages; Paper; 6 x 9 inches; $12.95

"Say *Yes* to life," the author continually invites in this welcome guidebook to the spiritual path. For anyone who has ever felt oppressed by the life-negative seriousness of religion, this book is a timely antidote. In language that translates the complex to the obvious, Desjardins applies his simple teaching of happiness and gratitude to a broad range of weighty topics, including sexuality and intimate relationships, structuring an "inner life," the relief of suffering, and overcoming fear.

Visit our websites at www.hohmpress.com and www.kalindipress.com

Other Titles of Interest from Hohm Press/Kalindi Press

DIRECTING THE POWER OF CONSCIOUS FEELINGS
Living Your Own Truth
by Clinton Callahan

Personal Growth / Emotions / Leadership
ISBN: 978-1-935387-11-4
370 pages; 50 b&w photographs; Paper; 6 x 9 inches; $29.95

This book is about feelings, and the ways that we, as individuals and as a culture, have numbed ourselves against them. It is about unleashing the possibility of conscious feelings to re-make our lives into what *really* matters to us. It introduces readers to the concept of the "personal numbness bar"—a measure set high by modern culture as a way of keeping everything "cool," under control, and consequently out of touch. This book provides the insight and the means for lowering that numbness bar. "You *can* feel more," the author asserts. You *can* regain the intelligence and energy of your feelings, so long denied and dressed up to appear acceptable.

• • •

RADIANT JOY BRILLIANT LOVE: *Secrets for Creating an Extraordinary Life and Profound Intimacy with Your Partner*
by Clinton Callahan

Relationships / Self-Help
ISBN: 978-1-890772-72-7
576 pages; Paper; 8 ½ x 11 inches; $29.95

This book challenges the deceptions about love and intimacy rampant in today's patriarchal culture. At the same time, it reveals a step-by-step process for discovering and living out alternative possibilities.

The author claims that even the "best" of our relationships are still generally basic level; what he calls "Ordinary Human Relationship." He asserts that two more domains remain to be explored: namely, Extraordinary Human Relationship and Archetypal Love. The book shows exactly how to enter these new domains, and how to stay there long enough to cultivate genuine intimacy, nurturance, excitement and satisfaction together.

Visit our websites at www.hohmpress.com and www.kalindipress.com

ABOUT THE AUTHOR

John Renesch is a businessman-turned-futurist living in San Francisco, an advisor, mentor and prolific writer on matters of leadership, organizational and social transformation, and the future.

Renesch has over four decades of experience as a business owner and entrepreneur. He's founded or co-founded a variety of companies, starting when he was eighteen years old. In the mid-1980s, after a period of deep personal introspection prompted by his call to work on matters of global importance, he left his chief executive position in the investment industry and embarked upon a new path.

From 1990 to 1997, he served as publisher and Editor-in-Chief of New Leaders Press, dedicated to publishing progressive business books and the periodical *The New Leaders*. In this role he oversaw the creation of twelve business anthologies on the subject of business and organizational transformation, which included the writings of over 300 visionaries. Among these visionaries were global leadership expert Warren Bennis, Gary Zukav (author, *The Seat of the Soul*), *One Minute Manager / Who Moved My Cheese* creator Ken Blanchard, Riane Eisler (author, *The Chalice and the Blade*), M. Scott Peck, MD (author, *The Road Less Traveled*), The Body Shop founder Anita Roddick, former Herman Miller CEO Max DePree, television genius Norman Lear, Harvard University's Rosabeth Moss Kanter, management guru Tom Peters, *Megatrends* series creators John Naisbitt and Patricia Aburdene, Stanford Business School Professor Michael Ray, and former USSR president Mikhail Gorbachev.

Renesch is now an independent global futurist, humanitarian, mentor/advisor, writer and keynote speaker on topics that integrate the subjects of work, human consciousness and positive scenarios for the future of humanity. He has also become a social activist, an advocate of social and organizational transformation and provocateur of a global awakening of the latent potentialities of the human race.

Prior to writing this book, he published thirteen books, including a novel, and hundreds of articles in futures journals, newspapers and magazines from around the world. His most recent book before this one was *Getting to the Better Future: A Matter of Conscious Choosing*. He publishes a free monthly newsletter called *The Mini-Keynote*. Here are some sample comments on his writings:

> "Effectively captures a spiritual renaissance taking place in the business world today." —Stephen R. Covey, author, *The 7 Habits of Highly Effective People.*

> "This perspective will be vital." —Fritjof Capra, author, *The Tao of Physics*, and *The Turning Point*

> "Don't skip this book." —*Entrepreneur Magazine*

> "John's book argues powerfully for business to play a leadership role in the transformation of our planet. It is an argument I can't resist. —Neale Donald Walsch, author, *Conversations With God*

As a keynote speaker, Renesch has presented to audiences in Tokyo, Seoul, Brussels, London, Sao Paulo, Porto Alegre, Zurich, Amsterdam, Port-of-Spain, Caracas, Gold Coast, Brisbane, Budapest and many cities throughout the Unites States and Canada. Here are some comments from his audiences:

> Ruth Otte, President, The Discovery Channel: "John Renesch eloquently illuminates a fresh, thoughtful, hopeful path."

> Warren Bennis, Distinguished Professor Emeritus, University of Southern California: "John is a wise elder who shines with wisdom."

> Rosa Alegria, Delegate, Ethos Institute 2006 Annual Conference (Brazil): "John enlightened the audience with his positive and healing message...one of the most remarkable moments of the four days."

> Carol Holding, Member, The Commonwealth Club of California: "John Renesch's address to our club...was timely and provocative. He makes you think!"

Perry Pascarella, Editor-in-Chief, *Industry Week* magazine: "John Renesch is a true visionary who sees the potential to rise above our failings and take the next step in human evolution before our system collapses."

Vitor Morgensztern, board member, World Business Academy, Brazil: "John addressed our "Meeting of Presidents"…and it couldn't have gone better. His clearness, perception and good humor enchanted and illuminated our invited members."

Michael Ray, Professor Emeritus, Stanford University School of Business, author: "John Renesch is a beacon lighting the path of the new paradigm in business."

Renesch offers private mentoring and coaching services to leaders, senior consultants and organizational executives from both the private and public sectors. He has been on retainer by several international organizations on a project basis. He is a member of the practitioner faculty for the Center for Leadership Studies, past member and project advisor of the World Future Society, current member and Inaugural Board Chair of the Shaping Tomorrow's Foresight Network, member of the *New Voice of Business* and Institute of Noetic Sciences and a founding Fellow of the international consortium The Global Collaborators' Alliance.

Renesch has been interviewed by *The Wall Street Journal*, *Forbes* (both Brazil and U.S.), *The Nikkei Financial Times* (Japan), *Business Week,* public radio's "Marketplace," CNBC-TV's Ron Insana on "Management Today Show," National Public Radio, *Chief Executive* and *Industry Week* magazines on the subject of consciousness and business. *The Futurist* magazine calls him a "business visionary."

See: www.thegreatgrowingup.com

ABOUT HOHM PRESS

Hohm Press is committed to publishing books that provide readers with alternatives to the materialistic values of the current culture and that promote self-awareness, the recognition of interdependence, and compassion. Our subject areas include parenting, religious studies, women's studies, the arts and poetry. Our affiliate, **Kalindi Press,** presents titles in the fields of natural health and nutrition, gender studies, and the acclaimed *Family and World Health Series* for children and parents.

Contact Information: Hohm Press, PO Box 31, Prescott, Arizona, USA; 928-778-9189; *hppublisher@cableone.net.*

Visit us at: *www.hohmpress.com* / *www.kalindipress.com*